DREAMS

WITH A

MESSAGE

DEVELOPING THE GIFT OF DREAM

INTERPRETATION

"I will give you the treasures of darkness and
secret riches of hidden places."
—Isaiah 45:3

DEBORAH KATHERINE SMITH

ISBN 978-1-63630-953-8 (Paperback)
ISBN 978-1-63630-954-5 (Digital)

Covenant Books, Inc.
11661 Hwy 707
Murrells Inlet, SC 29576
www.covenantbooks.com

To my husband, Dennis. Thank you for encouraging me to write this book. Thank you for pushing me out of my comfort zone. You are the man of my dreams. I am so very grateful to God for you and for bringing us together as one.

To all of my prayer warriors and friends that have prayed for me and for this book to come forth. You know who you are. To, especially, Cory Anna, my TAG group, Ginny, the Wednesday SSI Bible Study girls, and Chris (& friends)—thank you for holding me accountable to the end.

To my fellow dreamers. This book is written for you. May the pages come alive in your hearts and spirits. May you hear the Lord's voice in a new way and receive fresh revelation.

CONTENTS

INTRODUCTION

A man has joy by the answer of his mouth: and a
word spoken in due season, how good is it!
—Proverbs 15:23

One day, the Lord used an aggravating situation with my husband, Dennis, to get my attention. I was pouring out my heart to him, letting him know how I truly felt about something that was bothering me, and he answered with a "grunt." This prompted me to reword and rephrase my thoughts thinking maybe he didn't fully understand it all to which he then responded with something like, "That sounds great, babe," as he flicked the next channel on the TV set. Ugh. I was so furious! At that moment, I felt rejected and unimportant to him. He was not **listening** to me.

Alternatively, in **His** still small voice, the Lord spoke to me that very moment and told me that I did not like the way that **HE** was speaking to me either, and that I had not been listening to Him. Surely there was some kind of mistake here, so I sheepishly asked Him what He meant. He then said that I was rejecting *His attempts to speak to me*. He went on to point out that He had been "speaking" to me at night for a long time in dreams but that I had not been taking the time to inquire about them and I had thought of them as unimportant. He wanted me to embrace this form of communication that I had been neglecting. I have always had a very active dream life; sometimes even dreaming three or four dreams per night, but since I couldn't understand them, I had been dismissing them. With my head held low, I repented and told the Lord that I would make the effort to record my dreams and give them to Him to see what He might say. So I have been on a journey of seeking the Lord for insight and interpretation over the last thirty years.

I can honestly say that I have not been able to interpret every dream nor do I believe at all that every dream has been given by God. Thankfully, though, God is patient. He has encouraged me to continue to seek revelation in this area. He has challenged me not to give up when I don't have all of the answers. On the other hand, I have experienced life-changing events by seeing the interpretations through to the end. It has been so worth the effort. There has been the extraordinary, even phenomenal side, as stolen property has been recovered because of directions in dreams. Some dreams have aided in the selling of homes and businesses. In response to dreams, I have successfully been able to warn others of impending danger (before it happens), and there have also been joyful dreams of conception and good news. And yet there is also the ordinary, and most important of all, <u>practical side</u> to the messages in dreams that will light even the most mundane day. All of this has come about simply from my taking more seriously and pursuing God's way of "speaking" to me.

Do you sense that your dreams could have messages within them that are relevant to your daily life? Is it possible that God could be "speaking" to you in this way? My hopes are that this book will be a catalyst by which you (!), the reader, will become more active and responsive toward your own dreams and in your relationship with the Lord. My prayer is that you won't give up when you don't understand the meaning of your dream but that you will recognize the Lord's longing to speak to you and give you understanding. By embracing His great desire to answer you, you will be propelled to seek Him fully for more revelation. Do you REALLY want to hear what He has to say? I do! And I believe that if you are reading this that you long to hear Him more clearly as well. Take James's words to heart:

> Let perseverance finish its work so that you
> may be mature and complete, not lacking anything.
> If any of you lacks wisdom, you should ask God,
> who gives generously to all without finding fault,
> and it will be given to you. (James 1:4–5 NIV)

God does not want us frustrated and confused. He wants us to glean from His truths and from His interaction in our lives. He wants to answer our questions and give us direction, wisdom, and practicality. He wants to give us abundant life! "I am come that they might have life, and that they might have it **more** abundantly" (John 10:10, emphasis mine).

Throughout this journey, I will share many of my own dreams with their interpretations. Also, you will see the practical avenues and interesting twists of what has happened when I have ventured to respond to the dream's interpretation. Some dreams can be quite personal. And since I have a tendency to keep myself "private," these writings are bringing me out of my comfort zone, but it will be so worth it if you, the reader, can receive some helpful keys to assist **you** in unlocking some of the mysteries of decoding your own dream language.

We will look at many aspects of dreams; what to do with them, how to understand them more fully, how to respond to them, and what to do when they just don't make any sense at all. We will also look at a few biblical people and how God spoke to them through dreams. We will look at what was going on in their lives at the time of the dream. We will also focus on their responses to the way that God was speaking to them.

Let's get started. Do your best to read through the steps that I outline. Hopefully, this will not be boring (I'll try to keep it interesting with some juicy details and not put you to sleep...no pun intended). You may have the tendency to go right to the "interpretation" chapters but try not to skip the next couple of chapters; they are so very vital as they give you a foundation on which to build upon, keys to understanding your dreams, and practical steps to take in the process.

CHAPTER 1

GOD, PIZZA, OR ME?

> For my thoughts are not your thoughts, neither are
> your ways my ways, saith the Lord. For as the heavens
> are higher than the earth, so are my ways higher than
> your ways, and my thoughts than your thoughts.
> —Isaiah 55:8–9

Okay, this is where it can get a little hairy. I hope I don't lose you in this first chapter, but this is a necessary chapter as we need to look at establishing the origin of dreams.

I recently responded to a dream question online, and the writer had a dream which involved some sexual content. She wanted to know if her sexual dream could really be "from God." My short answer to her was, "Yes"; God can do ANYTHING He wants to. Period. **We** are the ones who are guilty of placing limitations on Him. If He doesn't seem to fit right inside of our tiny box that we've all nicely packaged up to put Him in, then we figure it "must not be **from Him**." The problem is He has this uncanny way of busting out of that box every time! We really need to take to heart that since **His ways are not our ways** (see above scripture), **then we have to keep ourselves open to what *might possibly be* His ways** (!), aka ways that **we** don't have a clue about.

I am positive that you are curious now and want to know what happened with the sexual dream. This dreamer had a sexual dream that involved her boss. She was troubled by it but curious about whether there was any meaning to the dream. I wrote to her and told her that it was quite possible that there was a message for her in it and that she should pray about it and ask the Lord about it. I suggested to her that maybe there was something that the Lord wanted to show her in regards to this person and maybe she should keep an open mind about it. I told her that sometimes sexual dreams can have messages in them and that the message is not about "sex" but more about something in regards to the relationship (of the people in the dream). She was very skeptical, but she said that she would pray about it. A couple of weeks later, she wrote back to me and excitedly shared that out of the blue, her boss came into her office to just chat one morning (something that he did not normally do). While they were talking, he began to offer some advice to her in regards to a stressful financial situation that she had been experiencing. This advice tremendously helped her, and she immediately was reminded of the dream. She never expected that her boss would be instrumental in regards to this financial problem, but it was obvious that the Lord used her boss's financial advice to answer her prayers.

I do not for a moment think that EVERY sexual dream is from the Lord or that there is necessarily a "message" in all of these kinds of dreams. My point here is to alert you to recognize that the Lord CAN use these kinds of dreams (and does) to speak to us.

Also, I personally believe that we live such busy lives that we don't always have (or take) the time to seek God. Therefore, it is only fitting, to me, that He would give us a dream with sometimes rather odd scenes and pictures in order to get **our attention** and commune with us. So where do we go from here in the "Is it from God or not" question?

In my dream journey, I chose to start with the idea that every dream could be from God. Now, mind you, I don't believe for a moment that every dream IS from God, but what I am saying is in order to learn which dreams are or aren't, I had to START with this notion and treat every dream this way in order to begin somewhere. If you start with this idea, then you aren't missing anything, and you can essentially learn as you go over time. As you go along in your dream journey, you WILL learn over time, and you will have a much better idea of whether it is a God dream, with a message in it, or not.

Dreams Are a Natural Part of Life

I am not a psychiatrist or psychologist. However, I do understand and believe that dreaming is a normal, natural part of life. I think that sometimes when we dream, we are sort of, for lack of a better word, getting cleaned out. It's like we are still processing things from the day, sort of, and dreams are a natural way for us to experience a release. Probably needful to many of us, dreams can help our bodies, minds, and emotions get rid of stored stress. As a society, we take in so much "stuff" from computers, cell phones, TV, work, family, and friends; there is a constant taking in of information and emotional/intellectual items. Dreams are just one way that we can gain a release from the clutter of these things that can stay harbored within. Therefore, **not every dream has a message**. I would certainly caution you about this and not to look for some kind of "direction" or "revelation" in every dream because that is just not going to be the case since regular dreaming is just a natural part of life.

Here are three scriptures that mention dreams as being a part of normal and natural life (having nothing to do necessarily with communication from God):

1. Ecclesiastes 5:3 says that we can recognize a fool's voice by (his/her) multitude of words. In this same verse, as a comparison, "dreams are said to come through a multitude of business." In other words, dreams, in general, can come when we have many cares, anxieties, or busyness.

2. Isaiah 56:10 in the Amplified Bible says, "[Israel's] watchmen are blind, they are all without knowledge; they are all dumb dogs, they cannot bark; dreaming, lying down, loving to slumber" (emphasis mine). This passage is referring to leaders who are blind, lazy, without ability, and who basically just sleep and dream. As if to say that, again, dreaming is a natural part of life and sleep.

3. Isaiah 29:7 and 8—God is speaking about those nations that fight against Jerusalem, and He is comparing them to a (bad) dream. In verse 8, He describes an example of a troubling or bad dream:

> It shall even be as when a hungry man dreams, and behold, he eats; but he awakes, and his soul is empty: or as when a thirsty man dreams, and behold he drinks; but he awakes, and behold he is faint, and his soul hath appetite:…so shall the multitude of all the nations be that fight against mount Zion.

> In other words, they will get nowhere, not accomplishing anything. They will be unfulfilled as the hungry and thirsty (man) who dreams of food and drink and doesn't receive any; as a bad dream without result.

Nightmares

When I was a little girl, I had nightmares. There were multiple times that I would awake in the middle of the night and be terrified of what I had just dreamed. These dreams were evil. They had no purpose. In addition, I watched A LOT of scary movies when I was growing up. I liked them. Do I believe that watching the scary movies affected my dream life? Yes, I do. I believe that whatever we "put in" is going to come out…in some kind of way. What we allow to come in through our eyes, ears, mouth, etc. affects us mentally, spiritually, and affects our overall behavior including our dream life.

Proverbs 4:20–27 says,

> My son, pay attention to what I say; turn your ear to my words. Do not let them out of your sight, keep them within your heart; for they are life to those who find them and health to one's whole body. Above all else, guard your

heart, for everything you do flows from it. Keep your mouth free of perversity; keep corrupt talk far from your lips. **Let your eyes look** straight ahead; fix your gaze directly before you. Give careful thought to the paths for your feet and be steadfast in all your ways. Do not turn to the right or the left; keep your foot from evil.

Luke 11:34 says, "**Your eye** is a lamp that provides light for your body. When your eye is good, your whole body is filled with light. But when it is bad, your body is filled with darkness."

Things that we watch on TV and/or movies, music we listen to, etc. can manifest in our hearts and minds and eventually turn into actions. I am not a prude. This is just a biblical principle that we can choose to apply to our lives or not. What we "take in" can greatly affect our dream life and does. If you are having regular nightmares and lots of soulful dreams that have no purpose, you need to monitor what you are taking in. Realize that there is a spiritual realm...both good and evil. Demonic forces are present and can affect your dream life, <u>particularly</u> if you are presently opening the door to this activity or even if somewhere in your past, you have opened it.

Ask the Holy Spirit to be your guide. Filter activities through Him. Take Philippians 4:8 to heart, which says, "Finally, brothers and sisters, whatever is true, whatever is honest, whatever is just, whatever is pure, whatever is lovely, whatever is admirable—if anything is excellent or praiseworthy—think about such things." If you truly apply this one scripture, you will find that your dream life (and life in general) will become free of "junk" both fleshly and soulish. It will then become easier to decipher what truly are God's messages and what are not.

I do want to comment that God will use what we might consider a "bad" dream to speak to us. In other words, dreams with a message can be troubling, even scary at times. They aren't always fluffy and fun. As you seek the Lord and ask Him for confirmation, you will begin to recognize the difference between a demonic "nightmare" dream and a God-given truthful, yet concerning, message dream.

Recognizing a God Dream—A Dream with a Message

I am going to set the stage for this real-life God dream. Take it in and really contemplate what was going on in the heart of this young man when he received his dream from God:

He loved her. They were engaged to be married. They had never experienced intimacy with one another, yet he finds out that she is pregnant. What could he do? What should be done? He feels his whole world is being turned upside down. Confused, bewildered, angry, helpless, hurt, but more than anything, at a loss...at a teetotal loss about what to DO. Abortion is not an option. He couldn't "run away," although he might have wanted to. There were no planes, then, for him to take off for a weekend. This was a serious dilemma.

He decides that the best plan for everyone would be to put her in hiding so that she wouldn't be disgraced (in their culture) and just call off the wedding. He is a good and morally righteous man. He wants to do the right thing. Maybe this is the answer...yes, this needs to be kept hidden. He doesn't want her to be embarrassed or humiliated.

I guess by now you know that I am describing Joseph in the New Testament. Have you ever really thought about him and what he went through during Mary's divine conception? We tend to focus more on Mary and her interaction with the angel Gabriel in Luke 1:26–38 (which is so miraculous, therefore, it truly gets our full attention.) The Bible tells us that God sent Gabriel to Mary...right into her room. They actually had a detailed conversation about the conception and how it would take place. He also gave her other information including her relative Elizabeth's pregnancy; details about what name to give her son, Jesus, and about His future kingdom. This is amazing! Profoundly miraculous and yet we are able to easily accept it, believe it, and know that it took place.

But do we ever really focus on Joseph? We need to. After all, the lineage of Jesus as laid out in Matthew 1:1–17 tells us that Jesus came through JOSEPH's line. I find that interesting that God didn't just say Mary but he says Joseph, the husband of Mary (Matt. 1:16), even though Joseph did not physically father Jesus in conception. It's easy, unfortunately, for us to read about these biblical figures and think that they had supernatural powers, like that they were somehow above us and unrelatable to our down-to-earth, sinful, crazy mixed-up lives. But the truth is that they were just like we are. Scared. Worried. Human. Pitifully human and really (!) in need of God just as much as we are today. So what does God do? How does He direct Joseph and show him the solution to his desperate situation? He chooses to speak to Joseph another way. He shows Joseph what He wants him to do **in a dream**. Let's look at it starting in Matthew 1:20.

The verse starts out with, "But while he [Joseph] thought on these things." I want to stop there for just a bit and tell you that God meets us in our everyday stuff when He speaks to us in dreams. He is so very near. He is right there in the middle of our icky, daily, doodad stuff! And He wants to help us with it. All of it. If we will let Him. When we do receive dreams that we think may have a real message for us, we need to keep in mind that most of the time they relate to us right where we are, and the message, many times, answers/directs us in regards to daily situations that we are facing that we have been praying about, wondering about, etc. So getting back to Joseph's situation, God knew that Joseph had a big decision to make, and He knew Joseph's thoughts and troubling concerns. So while Joseph was thinking about what to do, the Lord sent an angel who appeared to Joseph **in a dream**. This angel, described as "the angel of the Lord," told him not to be afraid of marriage to Mary and that the baby she was carrying was truly a Holy Ghost conception. The angel went on to confirm what Jesus's name should be, and the angel told him more about Jesus and the fulfillment of prophecy about Him. Joseph responded in obedience as we see in Matthew 1:24–25, "Then Joseph, **being aroused from sleep**, did as the angel of the Lord commanded him and took to him his wife, and did not know her till she had brought forth her firstborn Son. And he called His name Jesus."

Joseph paid attention to the dream. He made the decision to honor the instructions given in the dream.

Well, you might say, "If an angel spoke to me in a dream, I would do what it said also." I tend to disagree. The reason I disagree is because as a society, generally, we don't take dreams seriously. We certainly don't see them as a form of "communication" from God or even an angel, for that matter. Mostly, we laugh at our dreams and write them off as a funny story or tale. We attribute them to what we ate or drank the day before. What we have to realize is that God can use ANYTHING He wants to. He is God. We are not. And according to the Bible, there are twenty-one dreams recorded in which the dreamer(s) were receiving messages from God. On top of this, countless visions are recorded. Therefore, it behooves us to pay attention to our dreams and consider that there "could be" messages within them that may help us.

The dream that Joseph had was specific, and he knew what he was being told and he knew what it meant. The message was clear. He didn't need interpretation. This will not always be the case, of course. I wish it was. But it just isn't. The truth is that with most dreams, we just don't understand. We don't understand what the meaning could be or if there is even any meaning to it at all. Let's look at this a little further.

Over time, I have found a regular theme with dreams that have a message.

Distinguishing Dreams with a Message

I am speaking from the heart here. There isn't a scripture and verse for this next part, but it is, rather, personal pages taken from the book of my life (and dream journals). So… What differentiates a regular, normal dream from a special message (GOD) dream? Well, I have found that when there is a relevant message in the dream, there are several key elements. You could experience one or two of these elements with EVERY dream that you have, but what I have found is that when the dream has a message, I experience most of these, if not _all_ of them:

1. You go over and over the dream thinking about it for an extended amount of time (all day, days, weeks, months, or even years) and the _details of the dream stay with you_—you don't <u>easily</u> forget them.

2. The dream evokes strong emotions within you.

3. The dream seems real and is clear and many times colorful (as opposed to "fuzzy" dreams).

4. There is something about the dream that disturbs you so much that you just **know** it is important.

5. The dream can be reoccurring and/or you may have a similar dream with similar themes.

OKAY. Again, I am speaking from the heart and from personal experience. I would like to note an important key about dreams that are from God. These dreams have a PURPOSE. They have a message, and they have a result. Can they be preposterous? Yes, sometimes. Can they be confusing? Yes, sometimes. Can they be frightening? To be honest...yes, sometimes. This is not meant to discourage but to encourage you.

Let's look at the twenty-one different biblical dreams that I mentioned earlier, and what I want to point out is the intention or **purpose** God had in giving the dream. In other words, what is the end result? What was God conveying to the dreamer? This will help you see HIS WAYS and His "whys" in the dreams that HE gave. I have listed the scriptures where the dreams are located and then I have listed the results of the dream only. Hopefully, you will research the dream in its entirety in scripture, but at this point and with this list, I want you to mostly look at the **end result** of what God was accomplishing in giving the dream. Hopefully, this will give insight into some of the ways that He works with dreams that He gives. Look at the results only and see the outcome of the dream to the dreamer:

DREAM SCRIPTURE	RESULTS/PURPOSE OF DREAM
Genesis 20:3–7	God exposes a lie that's been told and warns of death if the truth isn't heeded.
Genesis 28:12–17	During a transition, God confirmed His presence, gave immediate direction, and future blessing.
Genesis 31:10–13	God gave specific direction as to when and where to physically move to.

Genesis 31:24	In the midst of a difficult time, God showed what kind of behavior should be displayed.
Genesis 37:1–8 and 9–11	God foretold of exaltation and honor.
Genesis 40:9–15 and 16–23	While imprisoned, God gave the outcome of the situation: their future fate.
Genesis 41:1–4 and 41:5–7	God showed the future of the economy.
Judges 7:13	God showed what the outcome of a battle would be before it was fought, which encouraged His people not to be afraid and move forward.
1 Kings 3:5–15	God had a request of the dreamer; God also granted a request with benefits.
Daniel 2	God showed the long-term future of kings, kingdoms, and Jesus, the King of kings. He also brought exaltation to his servants.
Daniel 4	God showed the need for repentance and humility.
Daniel 7	God showed coming kingdoms and the supreme reigning of His kingdom.
Matthew 1:18–24	God dispels fear, confirms marriage, Jesus, and the divine conception.
Matthew 2:12	God warned about danger in travel and gave directions to go home another way.
Matthew 2:13	God gave temporary moving instructions.
Matthew 2:19, 20	God gave further moving instructions.
Matthew 2:22	God gave even further moving instructions and a warning.
Matthew 27:19	God gives a troubling dream as a message from a wife to warn a husband about a current situation.

As you can see in these dream results, God is quite concerned about and very involved in the everyday lives of people. Some of the words to describe His ways in dream results are (He) encourages, warns, directs, reveals, rebukes, exposes, exalts, answers, confirms, foretells, and troubles us, when necessary. Bottom line: God has purpose in giving dreams. When it is truly a "God dream," there is a reason and a purpose. There is also, eventually, a result.

If I had my preference, I would go right into the interpretation part of dreams and skip this foundational chapter. But I have to tell you that it is more beneficial for you to understand that not all dreams are going to have messages in them. As we pay attention to our dreams and as we further our relationship with the Lord, we can recognize the difference between a "natural part of life" dream, a nightmare, and a dream with a message.

There's one other thought that I have to give you from this first establishing chapter. Most of the time, we receive direction from the Lord by means other than dreams. The Lord has given us His Word (the Bible) as our guide. He has also sent His precious Spirit (bought with the blood of Jesus) into our hearts to lead us and to guide us. And if that is not enough, He also provides "road maps" in our lives in the form of parents, pastors, teachers, spouses, bosses, counselors, friends, etc. who help point us in the right direction. I have been in Christian leadership for many years, and I have watched many Christians neglect these important resources that He has given us and, instead, turn to their most recent "dream" as their primary source of guidance. Frustrated and confused, this dreamer manipulates the dream by trying to understand every tiny detail. In addition, this dreamer spiritualizes all of it and then can go so far as to try and make it mean something that it totally doesn't mean in order for it to mean what they want it to mean. I urge you...do not be like this dreamer! Disaster will follow.

Ask the Lord **first** for direction in your life. Embrace whatever way He chooses to speak to you. The Bible, the Holy Spirit inside of us, counselors (people in our life), circumstances, etc. are the foundational and PRIMARY means that God has established to speak into our lives. Dreams are an additional way that He can speak into our lives and, I might go so far as to say, a *secondary* way. I know, I know. Here I have written a book about dreams and dream interpretation, and I am the one downplaying dreams! Not really. My point is that dreams from God are GREAT, but don't let them be your only ultimate directional guide in life. If dreams are one of the ways that HE has chosen to speak to you, seek **HIM** for the interpretation. If <u>He</u> gave the dream, then <u>He</u> has the interpretation. If you are willing to hear what He has to say and you are patient to allow Him to speak as He chooses, then He will bring clarification. And He will use many avenues to confirm His will and His leading.

So to summarize:

- Dreaming is a natural part of life. Not all dreams are "from God." Dreaming is a normal and natural way of cleaning us out from our daily activities. Not every dream has a message.
- Our dreams can be affected by what we "take in."
- Dreams from God have a message and a purpose.
- Pray for God's direction in your life and embrace His Word. Most of the time, we receive direction from the Lord by means other than dreams.

The next chapter is IMPERATIVE in your dream journey. My prayer is that you will read it and truly begin to implement it. In my opinion, it is the most important key to correct dream interpretation.

CHAPTER 2

WRITE THE VISION

He shall fly away as a dream, and
not be found; yea, he shall be chased
away as a vision of the night.

—Job 20:8

And the Lord answered me, and said,
"Write the vision, and make it plain upon
tables, that he may run that reads it."

—Habakkuk 2:2

In order to receive ALL that you can from your dream, it is crucial that you **write it down**. Record it, in some way. If you get nothing else out of this book, PLEASE GET THIS. Write your dream down or record it in some way!

With the many technological means that are available today, there are several different options as to how to record, including speaking it into an electronics device or phone. But for me, personally, I find that writing out the dream has been the best way to capture it. Make sure that you have a notebook or journal and pen within arm's reach of your bed. I can't tell you the number of times that I have failed to make provision for this and wished that I hadn't. If I don't write it down immediately upon waking, inevitably, the phone will wake me up, the dog will bark, or some random distraction will come along and cause me to forget some of the clearer details. And, yes, there have been several times that I have woken up in the wee hours of the night thinking that I could remember a dream that I was just having, only to find that later when I fully awoke it has "flown away" as our chapter scripture mentions (Job 20:8).

You may keep a separate journal to record your dreams. Sometimes, I record them separately, but most of the time, I record both the dreams and the notes from my quiet time with the Lord together in the same journal. I have found that many times the scriptures that I am reading during the time of the dream will actually go along with and coincide with the messages within the dreams. I will share more on this in Chapter 6.

Next (and please get this!), follow Habakkuk 2:2…write the dream and MAKE IT PLAIN. Record the date. Try to record EVERY DETAIL that you have seen, heard, etc. Writing the dream down is imperative. You will think you can remember it, but usually you can't. The same goes with DETAILS; take the time to write everything down and make the DETAILS very plain. Don't say to yourself, "Oh, I don't need to write that down because I could never forget that." You **will** forget it, so DEFINITELY *write it down <u>exactly as you received it</u>*.

I have found that as I awaken and consider the dream, what I may "think" is the most important detail may end up not to be. It is sometimes a more minor detail that triggers the interpretation, so writing <u>all</u> of the details down is crucial. Ironically, some dreams are about future events. I have had numerous times where the dream is about something that is coming down the road. Therefore, it is important to write it ALL down because you may need something from the dream's details to aid in future meaning.

I want to tell you a personal true story (that happened to me) which will illustrate the importance of recording details:

At the time, Dennis and I had a second home in the beautiful mountains of Western North Carolina. There is a serene lake not far from our home that has a popular walking path surrounding it. For years, we have taken our dog, family members, and friends to this spot for relaxation and exercise as the path is over two miles long. One sunny day, I decided to take our dog and go for some exercise.

We had gotten almost halfway around and noticed that there weren't too many people out that day. In the distance I could see a man waving his arms as if he was either trying to say "hello" or just trying to get my attention. I looked behind me to be sure he was not flagging someone else, but there was no one else behind me.

As my dog and I got closer, I noticed that he moved closer and closer to a circular group of hedges; he was still kind of waving his arms. Since a lot of people walk their dogs there, I then thought that maybe he had a dog with him that I could not see and maybe something was wrong (with his dog). Next, he either went behind or within this area of shrubbery—it was hard to tell from where we were—but we were getting closer and just about to come upon the area where he was. He hadn't come out of the area, so I glanced in the direction of the hedges, and what do you think I saw? Everything that I wasn't supposed to! Yep, he was standing there in "exposition," if you get my drift!

His plan, evidently all along, was to get my attention and keep my attention so that I would look his way as we passed the hedged area. I immediately walked as fast as I could to the nearest public area and called Dennis. Dennis told me to stay in the public area and he would call the police. He described my location to the authorities, and within minutes, the man was arrested. The police then gave me a form and told me to write down everything that had just taken place. I was encouraged to write it as detailed as I could…yuck! The arresting officer told me that this could most likely end up in court because the guy was denying that he did it. The policeman wanted to know if I would agree to be in court and pursue this, which, of course, I agreed to. This guy just didn't know who he tried to tangle with. I am not the kind of person to let things like this go. All I could think about were the many young women who jog and walk around this beautiful lake and how peaceful it is. If my involvement could help stop criminals such as this from continuing their "activities," then I had to DEFINITELY pursue the court situation.

Anyway, fast-forward to approximately nine months later when this case has finally come to court. I am sitting in the court room quite nervous waiting for our case to be called. Like I said, this is in

North Carolina, and I have no clue about court stuff as it is, but this is also in a state that we do not primarily reside in, so I felt definitely out of place.

I got called to the stand, and the man's attorney began asking me detailed questions in regards to what his client was wearing that day. I had neglected to get a copy of what I had written for the police report, so I had to recall everything from memory. Oh, sure, there were certain things that I could remember VERY well, but his attire was not one of them!

Also, when the attorney asked me to go over the incident step by step, I remembered that he was waving his arms, but I had forgotten the part where he was moving closer and closer to the bushes. This attorney was actually using my own words and my neglect to refresh myself of those words AGAINST ME to convince the judge that I had made this whole story up since I couldn't recall all of the minute details. I could feel myself getting angry; it had never even occurred to me that he might be found not guilty! Thankfully, the arresting officers were there and testified, and, double thankfully (!), there was other evidence against this guy that they had which implicated him. He was found guilty. I learned a large lesson that day. If I ever have to go to court again for any reason, I will be sure and get a copy of the police report and go over all of the details!

Keeping this story in mind, I hope that you are convinced that the details are important to record when you are writing out your dream because forgetting them can sabotage the outcome. Bottom line: Make sure you have the tools at hand that you need to record the dream and write all of the details so that you can go back over them later.

While we are touching on the importance of details, I want to STRONGLY reiterate. Record EVERY detail that you remember. Even those that you *may not like*! This is an important tip for you and one that I feel everyone struggles with. In helping others to interpret their dreams, I have found that people will tell me a portion of the dream but will tend to leave certain things out. **Many times, the part that is left out of a dream is a part that the dreamer doesn't personally "like" or sometimes that they don't understand**. But, in actuality, these uncomfortable parts are many times the **key** that unlocks the dreams' message! I encourage you to always record the dream in its entirety with *every* detail that you can remember.

Next, do not try and interpret as you write; that can come later. For now, it is important that you thoroughly <u>record it as you received it</u> without deciphering it yet so that you don't miss anything. That even means the "weird" stuff that doesn't make sense at the moment. The setting, colors, shapes, numbers, people, animals, etc., all of the details that you can remember and how the dream went from start to finish. **Just as you received it, record it**. After you've completed writing it, then record the tone of the dream; how it made you feel or any thoughts that you had during the dream. If you find that you can't remember it all, just write everything that you can remember.

With dream interpretation, you have to decide ahead of time that you are going to focus on the positive and not be held back from the negative factors; things that you don't understand or portions that you can't quite remember fully.

As an example of recording everything even when it makes no sense, I want to share...

The Weird Word Dream—I had this dream over twenty years ago. This was a "short" dream, and, by the way, short dreams sometimes pack the most punch, so don't overlook them! I dreamed that I heard a voice telling me very casually, "You need to take acidophilus." I didn't see a person in the dream, but it was like I was in a room and they were behind me talking to me. This is all that they said. End of dream.

The next morning, I wrote this dream down and spelled the weird word that I heard the best that I could. I asked the Lord to show me if this was such a thing. That was about it. I had no idea if it existed or if I had even remembered the word correctly, but I just wrote it like it sounded in the dream. Later, that day, I remember asking someone if they had ever heard of it, and my friend said that it sounded like an ingredient in yogurt. I researched it and found that my spelling was off but that the word, *acidophilus*, was found in yogurt and its primary use was to help protect the body against

harmful bacteria, parasites, and other organisms. It helps with digestion, which I have always had an extreme problem with!

I felt that the Lord was telling me that I needed to incorporate
yogurt into my diet. So I tried eating a serving of yogurt once a day,
and I began to see a major difference with my digestion. Mind you,
this was over twenty years ago…well, before the "yogurt craze" that
we see today. So needless to say, I eat yogurt on a regular basis (even
to this day!) and no more digestion problems. What a simple thing
(!), but if I had brushed the dream off as being too "weird" or not
understandable, I would have missed the Lord's practical help with
my problem. Okay, back to the steps of recording the dream:

After recording, now you can "run" with it (see the scripture
at the beginning of this chapter Habakkuk 2:2), as you read and
pray over it. You can highlight or underline or make notes about the
things that especially stand out to you. Ask the spirit of God to speak
to your heart. Ask Him to show you if this dream is from Him and
tell Him you are willing to hear what He has to say.

"Even the Spirit of truth whom the world cannot receive,
because it sees him not, neither knows him: but you know him: for
he dwells with you, and shall be in you" (John 14:17). Seek God
FIRST for revelation about the dream. Resist going to the internet,
your best friend, a dream book, etc. until you have sought the Lord
first. Yes, I advocate using resources to aid in interpretation (i.e. this
book), but that is after I have invited the Lord to speak to my heart.
Write down anything and everything that you feel He might be saying. Keep in mind that the Lord wants you to understand and "he is
not the author of confusion, but of peace" (1 Cor. 14:33).

Sometimes, I get absolutely nothing. Sometimes, I feel that He
is leading me to read certain scripture or He may bring a portion of
a scripture to my mind, and when I read it, then there will be more
insight that He gives. Other times, I find that I just won't get an
answer right when I want it, and I have to be very patient. In addition, timing is everything, and it might even be that it just isn't time
for the interpretation quite yet. Note: You will not like the having
to be patient part because you will feel compelled to find an answer

to the mystery, but I urge you to give God TIME to speak. This may mean days, weeks, or even sometimes years.

This is a key part to the entire dream journey; you can't give up. You really have to work out the interpretation. You have to be patient. Sometimes it can be quite easy, and other times it can be a horrendous struggle. Be patient with yourself (and with God).

I have had to wait and give God time to speak and gotten nothing on many occasions. I will leave it alone for a while and come back to it later, only to find nothing again. Other times, I have come back to it, and it's like a light just comes on and I know exactly what the dream means. This can be frustrating, but this is the "make or break" part of dream interpretation, and this is where the Lord and I have wrestled. This is where you will wrestle too, but it is so worth it.

You know getting back to the "basics" in life sounds so simple, but the truth is that it is quite life-changing. Many years ago, my mom shared a scripture with me that has helped me time and time again in everyday life. The scripture is the first part of Psalms 116:6, "The Lord preserves the simple." The Lord **preserves the simple**. In other words, simplicity lasts. It "keeps." There is less hassle when things are kept simple. Less complicated things tend to last longer, and keeping things simple means that you take the difficulty out of the picture and you are left with the true meat or heart of the matter...the part that is important; the part that lasts. Keep this basic thought in mind when interpreting also. *Simplicity* is key. God is so VERY PRACTICAL. We are the ones who try to spiritualize everything, and we end up sabotaging the dream result by trying to make it something that it absolutely just isn't!

I want to share a story about over-spiritualizing. I respond with dream advice, on occasion, online to a reputable Christian dream website. One dreamer, in particular, had been having dreams for years about different babies. In each dream, the dreamer was struggling with caring for the baby. The dreamer never seemed to be handling the baby right or giving it what it needed. She was constantly trying to "fix" a baby situation, but she never could, and sometimes the situation was even becoming worse with the babies' life or health in danger. I read this dream and watched how different people were responding online with things like, "Babies mean a new ministry" or "Babies can mean something new is coming in your life." Sure, babies can represent A LOT of different things, including the thoughts of the responders. The key is to seek the Lord and not to just try and plug in a "baby" (or anything else) as being symbolic of something until you have sought the Lord first.

My response to this dreamer (after praying) was that she was taking on responsibilities that were not hers to take on. In the meantime, she was finding it hard to care for the true responsibilities that she should be focusing on. I felt that the Lord was saying that she was trying to be a "fixer" and that He wanted to bring her freedom from the origin of feeling the need to take on responsibilities that weren't hers to take on.

The Lord is so practical, and I will reiterate this again and again in these pages. Why? Because He has had to tell ME this again and again. We want SO BADLY to receive direction from the Lord, and because we can be so very impatient, it can be tempting to try and "make" something happen in our lives by manipulating the details of a dream into what we **want** them to mean. When this happens, disaster follows. Resist the urge to "spiritualize" and **manipulate** the dream to "mean something." Bottom line: Ask the Lord. Seek <u>Him</u>. If <u>He</u> gave the dream, then He has the interpretation. If you are willing to hear what He has to say and you are patient, He will show you and bring clarification.

So to summarize where we are so far:

1. <u>Record</u> the dream <u>in detail</u> just as you remember it.
2. Write down or underline the highlights, as well as the feelings and thoughts that stand out to you.
3. <u>Ask the Lord</u> for the interpretation and then <u>listen</u> to His answer.
4. Be patient. Don't give up if you don't get an answer right away.
5. Resist the urge to "over-spiritualize" and manipulate the dream.

CHAPTER 3

DREAM LANGUAGE

It is the spirit that quickens [makes alive]; the
flesh profits nothing: the words that I speak
unto you, they are spirit and they are life.
—John 6:63

I LOVE the rain. Seriously. I actually look forward to it. The air has
that crisp, rainy smell that makes me almost sneeze. The clouds take
over the sky and are sometimes dark and gloomy-looking and other
times grayish-white. The wind picks up and is followed by thunder
and crackling lightning. But all of this makes me feel comforted.
When it finally rains, I relax. Many times, when it is raining, I go out
on our back-screened porch with a good book and cuddle up to read.
Usually, I end up napping. I love it! My outdoor plants love it too
and benefit so phenomenally from the rain's nutrients making them
vibrant and fresh. Yes, that is a good word…refreshing. That is what
rain is to me, and it truly is my favorite weather element even more
so than sunny, clear days.

Therefore, if I dreamed about rain, it would be a <u>great</u> dream,
to me. And the more it would rain (in a dream), the more I would
like it! Even if the dream itself wasn't necessarily pleasant BUT it was
RAINING in the dream, then that is a good sign to me because of **my
love for rain**.

Similarly, if I dreamed about something in regards to plumbing, it would remind me of business or money. Why would that be? My husband and I own a plumbing business, so I would automatically relate a plumbing dream to our business/money or something involving it or the aspect of it.

So why am I bringing up rain and plumbing, etc.? Because I am showing you things that are in my dream language. In order to understand your dreams, you need to realize that God speaks to you in a language that YOU can understand. With these concepts in mind, I want you to see that dream language is **personal**. My goal is to educate you as we go along so that you can decode and understand your OWN dreams. And to do that, you need to start recognizing *your* dream language. To further investigate dream language, let's look at a biblical example of personal dream language for Peter, one of the disciples.

In Acts 10:10, Peter was shown a life-changing vision from the Lord. Jesus, when he arose, appeared to his disciples (Peter being one of them) and told them "that repentance and forgiveness of sins will be preached in His name to all nations, beginning at Jerusalem" (Luke 24:46, 47 NIV). Well, the disciples certainly began to see repentance preached, and they saw many other phenomenal things including

- three thousand souls were saved (see Acts 2:41),
- physical healings were taking place (see Acts 5:16),
- Stephen was stoned (see Acts 7:59),
- great persecution arose and the church was scattered (see Acts 8:1 and 4), and
- Peter prayed for Dorcas who then arose from the dead (see Acts 9:40, 41).

The disciples were doing what Jesus told them to do, and their lives were literally turned upside down. Thus far, they had seen all of these mighty things happen, but up until now, they had ONLY preached repentance to the **JEWS**, not to "all nations" as Jesus had originally said to them (with the exception of Philip who went to the Samaritans who were "half breed"—one-half Jew and one-half Gentile).

In Acts 10:10, Peter is going up to his rooftop to pray, and he is starving. While his food is being prepared, he sees a **vision**. He sees the heavens opened and something like a great sheet lowered by the four corners descending to the earth. Within the sheet were "all manner of" clean and unclean animals and birds together. Then, Peter is told to "rise, kill, and eat." Peter's response was to say, "Surely not, Lord. I have never eaten anything impure or unclean." (Keep in mind that this was something that Peter had staunchly been brought up to adhere to.) Then God tells him not to call anything impure that HE has made clean. This was done three times before the sheet was received up to heaven again. (Okay, I have to say that if I had that dream about birds and animals in a sheet and I was told to eat them…um, I would seriously laugh and be looking for the nearest Outback restaurant or something along those lines!) But Peter knew what the animals/birds referred to. He was being shown something that **he** could relate to. Peter was hungry, and the Lord was giving him a picture in **his** dream language in regards to clean and unclean food. God is speaking to him about a major change in his life in regards to what is clean and unclean. The Lord is using clean and unclean food as an example to get his attention. So now, the scripture says that Peter is "inwardly perplexed" as to what the vision which he had seen might mean (Acts 10:17).

IMPORTANT TIP: I love this word *perplexed* because it is a great description of what you feel when you have a dream that truly has a message for you. It is normal to feel this way. And I love that the Bible states that Peter had this feeling about the vision's meaning! It is such an encouragement to me (and YOU!) that you will feel this way, and it is truly **okay and normal to feel this way**!

Let's play out Peter's vision to see what happens next. When the vision ends, within minutes, the Lord tells Peter that three men are in the yard asking for him and that he is to go down there and go travel with the men. Peter, just having seen this vision <u>three</u> times, is now looking at <u>three</u> men sent to him from a <u>Gentile</u> man, Cornelius, who wants to hear what Peter has to say about God. Now Peter is beginning to put two and two together with the vision, so, ultimately, he makes the trek with the men to meet Cornelius and tells him and the people who are with him about Jesus.

Peter realized that the vision was symbolic; it appeared to be about clean/unclean food, but he now knows that the Lord was really showing him about His acceptance of ALL mankind (clean and unclean). Peter needed to be shown this in a special way because this was a very new concept for him, and, evidently, the Lord was preparing him against being resistant. Peter's life revolved around Jewish tradition and a good amount of intolerance regarding the Gentiles. Peter's first words when he began to speak about the vision (vs. 34) were, "I now realize how true it is that God does not show favoritism."

In Acts 10:45, we are told that the believing Jews were astonished that the gift of the Holy Spirit was being poured out EVEN ON GENTILES. Peter wasn't astonished, though, because God had prepared him the day before with a beautiful picture message (vision) that he was able to comprehend and respond to as he became the first disciple to preach the gospel to the Gentiles! All because God had opened his heart to receive Gentiles as being "clean" in His eyes and the avenue He used to speak to Peter with was a **vision**!

Hopefully, you can see the dream language that spoke to Peter. Maybe you are even looking at your own dreams a little differently. Now, I want to share a personal dream with you that is a good example of this "dream language" concept. I will also share with you the interpretation and how I achieved it. Incidentally, we will also add another "step" to our basic list, so pay close attention to an additional step that will be pointed out:

The Blue Purse Dream—In this dream, I was shopping for a quality blue leather purse. I didn't find one at the store I was shopping at, but I made another trip on another day back to the same store and asked for the same employee to help me look again. They had other colors but not blue. I don't know why I returned to the same store, but I remember thinking that since they had so many purses, maybe we just hadn't looked hard enough. The employee finally found a blue knockoff purse that was nylon (not leather); it wasn't at all what I wanted, and it was starting to unravel. At the end of the dream, I knew that I could settle for what they had, but I wouldn't be happy unless it was a blue purse, and it had to be leather. I even looked at some of the other shoppers who were in the store, and I noticed that their purses were leather also, so the need for it to be BLUE and for it to be LEATHER really stood out to me in the dream. It was obvious that I needed to shop somewhere else and that I wasn't going to find the blue leather purse at that particular store no matter how hard I tried. Also, the store was sort of divided and had electronic/stereo stuff in a portion of it; it was half boutique and half electronic. Lastly, I felt like I was getting on the employee's nerves that was trying to help me. She thought I was being too picky, but I just knew what I wanted. End of dream.

Note: The above dream, as all of the dreams that I write out personally in this book, will be written out in full detail. The details are important in the overall message of the dream, but be careful not to "pick apart" each detail and try to make something out of it that it isn't. I record them, though, just as I explained in the previous chapter. We will work through what to do with them (or not) as we go along in these interpretation chapters.

My Steps of Interpretation: The next morning, after writing the dream out and asking the Lord for insight, I focused on the blue leather purse because it was the central object of the dream.

1. The first inclination when interpreting dreams is to treat the dream like it is literally something that is happening or that is going to happen. So I thought, maybe I need a blue purse, and I do love leather. However, I have learned by experience that some dreams can be literal, meaning true to fact or actual. But in this case, I really didn't feel the dream was literally about finding a purse but that it was more symbolic and that it wasn't literally about a purse but that there was a **message** within the dream.

2. I underlined the blue leather purse, and I underlined my determination to find a blue leather purse and not settle for less than that. Also, it was interesting to me that I kept trying to find this purse at this particular store. I felt that there

was more going on in this dream than just my wanting a blue purse, so I reread the dream several times and I wrote under the dream what I felt the <u>message</u> of it was, which is:

What I thought the message was: *I am searching for something specifically important that I need, but I am searching in the wrong place for it. I don't think that what I am searching for is wrong, but I am looking for it in the wrong place—it is <u>not there.</u>*

OUTCOME OF DREAM: Okay, so here's what happened:

In real life and later that same day after having the dream, one of our plumbers (an employee) came to me and expressed concern about another newly hired employee. We were trying to train the new employee to fill a certain niche in our business, but his abilities were seriously lacking in the area that we were training him in. The employee that came to me had been one of the trainers, and he had spent days training this new guy. The employee pointed out confidentially what the new employee lacked, but he also pointed out that the new employee had a tremendous ability in another area, and he suggested that we steer him toward this other ability. BINGO! My dream! The message! I went back to the dream and looked at the message again. It became clear to me that the dream was about our business and about our looking for this newly hired employee to be something that he just couldn't be.

Just so you understand, ALL of our plumbing business vans, the uniform shirts, our logos, etc. are BLUE. **The very same shade of blue as the blue purse that I was looking for in the dream.** And it being a blue **purse** (in reference to money) speaks to me because of our income/business. MY dream language! The dream was about our plumbing business. Let's continue.

We could have continued to train him in the area that we started out in trying to make him be a "blue leather purse" (profitable in a particular area), but it would have been a potentially disastrous situation because he just wasn't a "blue leather purse" in this area and we couldn't make him be one! We kept trying to train him over and over again in the same way in this area (remember my dream in that I was going back to the same store and to the <u>same employee</u> looking for the same result?), but he didn't have the qualities we desired and that we were looking for him to have. No blue leather purse there!

After realizing this, we took the advice of our plumber and moved this new employee into an area that he **is** gifted at. (Also, to note, I won't get involved in all of the details but the one-half electronic part of the purse store did mean something to me, and it had to do with this employee and his inability to perform certain technical aspects of the job we were trying to train him in.) We were trying to make him be the "blue leather purse" when he just wasn't. This brought great clarity to us and great peace to this new employee. This was a beautiful revelatory dream in a *language* that I understood. This dream provided practical help and direction for us at a time that we didn't really know that we needed it, but GOD KNEW. There was purpose and an outcome to this dream!

Let's look further at the next step that I am adding to our list: *Determining what the **message** of the dream is.*

Many times, when you perform this step or know this step, you have the interpretation lock, stock, and barrel and you need no further clarity. In this case, I felt that I knew what the message was, but there was more symbolic revelation that came and that made the whole dream become alive to our present situation with our new employee and tied the message together with the details of the dream. For me, it was like the light came on and that is about the best way that I can describe the feeling that you have when you get the complete interpretation. The light comes on and you have a full understanding of what the dream means. But going back to the dream and writing out what I thought was the **message** was a major key to help unlock the dream's meaning for me.

Hopefully, by now you are considering the different aspects of your own dream language. Keep in mind that God is personal in His relationship with each and every one of us, and He has a personal dream "language" with you that you can understand and relate to. Sometimes the dream will be literal, and other times it will be symbolic. Regardless of its nature, the dream is tailored for you and is being given to help YOU in a practical way. Most of the time, it is pertinent for right now, not something out in la-la land. Embrace the fact that God loves you and wants to get personal with you showing you down-to-earth things that will help you in your daily life.

IMPORTANT TIP: Let me reiterate the above. In relation to personal dream language and the message, I have to say that I have learned that MOST of the time, the dream is for and/or about you. Even though other people or things could be the main subject of the dream, the **message** is meant for YOU. There can be exceptions to this where you will dream and have messages for other people, and we will talk about them in the next chapter. But you will save yourself and others (!) a lot of frustration if you keep in mind that God is a personal God, and He is giving the dream TO YOU, FOR YOU, and most of the time, ABOUT YOU or about a situation that involves YOU! I will say that personally, most of the dreams that I have received are about very present things in my life at the time of the dream. On several occasions, I have dreamed of futuristic events. Also, I have dreamed of past things, but usually the Lord is bringing them to me in order to bring healing or revelation for something that I am experiencing presently.

Dream study and interpretation can be quite subjective and intangible. Therefore, it is important that you have some concrete and tangible steps that you use to help in your interpretation. So I want to go back over the basic list from the last chapter and add step #6 from this chapter. This list will give you a true and fool-proof guide to go by for the future as you dream and are looking for the dream's meaning. I use this list literally daily. So here it is again with the added step:

1. Record the dream in detail just as you remember it.
2. Write down or underline the highlights, as well as the feelings and thoughts that stand out to you.
3. Ask the Lord for the interpretation and then listen to His answer.
4. Be patient. Don't give up if you don't get an answer right away.
5. Resist the urge to "over-spiritualize" and manipulate the dream.

6. Begin to recognize your dream language and write out what you think to be <u>the message</u> in the dream, keeping in mind that God speaks to you in a language that YOU can understand. Most of the time, the dream is for/about YOU.

CHAPTER 4

IS IT LITERAL OR IS IT SYMBOLIC?

It is the glory of God to conceal a thing, but the
honor of kings is to search out a matter.

—Proverbs 25:2

God hides himself from us because He wants us to SEEK HIM

I really liked playing hide-and-seek when I was little. It was so much fun to me to hide in a strategic place that no one would ever think about finding me in. It could get to be a boring game when it was obvious where someone was because their leg was sticking out or they were giggling. But when you searched and searched and couldn't find the hidden person and it was a challenge, then that was when the game became really fun. I believe that God is like this at times. He seemingly hides Himself so that we will go after Him and discover Him in a new way.

Discerning and interpreting dreams can be like hide-and-seek. There is a measure of seeking that has to take place. Basically, you have to determine first:

1. Is the dream **literal** (*actual*)?
2. Is the dream **symbolic** (*represents something other than what appears*)?

Deciding if the dream is literal or symbolic is truly half of the battle.

Of the twenty-one biblical dreams (not including visions but dreams only), ten of them are literal with the remaining eleven being symbolic. If I compare this to my own dream experiences, I would agree that about one-half the time, my dreams are literal, and the other half of the time they are symbolic. My first instinct is usually to question this aspect of the dream: literal or symbolic? If it is a literal dream and you are aware of the meaning, then you don't have to look quite as hard to find the "message." Symbolic dreams are the ones requiring finding a message, and we will look at those more closely in the chapters ahead as they can be a little tricky to discern. Let's look at literal dreams first.

When you are given a literal dream, you may know right away that it is factual/actual. Sometimes, though, you may not know, and it may take a day or a week or some amount of time before something happens and you actually then realize that the dream was literal! (Again, another so important reason to WRITE IT DOWN so you can go back to it and look at the details. But enough harping on that for now.)

Literal dreams can be about many things. I want to share an example of a literal dream from the Bible. This particular dream is actually the very first dream that is recorded in the Bible, so it will be interesting to look at. Taken from Genesis 20, after Sodom and Gomorrah were destroyed with fire, Abraham and his wife Sarah begin journeying south to a land called Gerar, whose king was named Abimelech. Abraham, out of fear for his life, decides to lie to this king and tells him a partial truth. Abraham's thinking (as we see in verse 11) is that this land is not a God-fearing land, so Abraham surmised that the king would kill him in order to take Sarah as his wife because of her beauty. Abraham decides to tell King Abimelech that Sarah is his sister, and, sure enough, with this information, the king takes Sarah to become his. (In reality, Sarah is *partially* Abraham's sister because they have the same father but not the same mother; she is his half-sister, but she is ALSO Abraham's **wife**, a fact that Abraham failed to mention to the king.)

God speaks to King Abimelech in a dream and says to him, "You are a dead man because of the woman whom you have taken as your own, for she is a man's wife." Furthermore in the dream, Abimelech and the Lord have a discussion about the situation, but the Lord's final word is still the same in verse 7, as He tells Abimelech, "Restore to the man his wife; for he is a prophet, and he shall pray for you, and you shall live; and if you do not restore her, know that you shall surely die, you, and all that are yours."

This was a very literal and sobering dream that King Abimelech had. There was nothing symbolic or subjective to it. He was clearly instructed by the Lord as to what was going on in his life and also as to what he had to do about it. I find it intriguing that as in this dream and several other biblical dreams, the Lord is plainly speaking to people in the dream. We are not told whether or not there were any faces or pictures or scenery, etc., but I tend to think that there was. Of course, I do not KNOW that there was.

I guess my thoughts are just that I have experienced so many dreams where it was quite clear that the Lord was speaking to me and showing things in my life. If you had asked me later to put what I experienced in written form, I may have just said that the Lord spoke to me and not included any picture details because those wouldn't have stood out to me, only what was said. Please understand that I am not trying to add anything to what happened in Abimelech's dream. I am just saying that it is possible that there were more visual aids to the dream (background, scenery, etc.) but that what really mattered and spoke to Abimelech was what was captured in the Scripture…the *words* that the Lord spoke to him. The bottom line is God did speak to him and gave him instructions, and his life was changed immediately.

Abimelech obeyed and did, indeed, address the situation with Abraham. Abraham prayed for him. Abimelech returned Sarah to Abraham along with one thousand pieces of silver, sheep, oxen, and even servants. God restored Abimelech's household and healed them because the Scripture says that the Lord had closed fast all of the wombs in Abimelech's household, because of Sarah, Abraham's wife. This was a very literal dream for a very literal situation.

I am now going to share five personal literal dreams and their consequences. I would like to note that as I share the details of what later happens after these dreams take place, my hopes are that you will glean from them and especially notice God's WAYS and what some of the purposes of the dreams were so that this will help you better understand the "why" and "how" of literal dreams and their results.

Five Literal Dreams and Their Results

Dream 1. Background Information First

Many years ago, I had a male keeshond dog named "Eli." Eli was a very friendly, stately dog. He had a beautiful long outer coat with shades of gray, black, and white. He also had a large, fluffy, curved tail. He was very smart and had lots of personality. I had him for a few years, and then one day when I went out to feed him, he was gone. We scoured the neighborhood and finally found him romping around in someone else's yard. We brought him home back to his fenced-in backyard. We had absolutely no idea how he had gotten out. A few weeks later, this happened again, but this time it took over a week before he finally came home on his own. Again, we had no idea how he was getting out, and we even wondered if possibly mischievous children in the neighborhood could be opening the gate and letting him out of the fence. After a third time of the same thing, I had a dream. This particular dream is one that I will refer to throughout this book as a *picture dream*.

A **picture dream** is not some great philosophical thing but rather my own description of a dream where you only see a PICTURE, and there is no movement or sound or anything else in the dream. This kind of dream is like a still image or a photograph. You just see what is there, and the dream is very short, but what you are seeing is deeply inscribed in your mind. You wake up the next morning and that image is just there, and you know there is something important about it. It is just like an *intense* imprint. Sometimes it can be in color and sometimes black-and-white. Regardless, it leaves an indelible image in your mind and spirit, and you know that it has deep meaning.

Here is the picture dream that I had:

The Missing Dog Dream—In the dream I saw (in real life) where the fence in our backyard met the edge of our home. The fence actually butts up to the house on either side, but in the dream, I was being shown the <u>left-hand</u> side of where it meets the house. End of dream.

I woke up the next morning and knew this dream had to do with Eli. How did I know it had to do with Eli? Well, I had been asking the Lord for answers about how he was getting out. Another reason that I knew that it had to do with Eli was because just the fence itself reminded me of him. The fence was there in order to keep him in, and I could think of no other reason to be dreaming about the fence unless it had to do with our dog.

After having the dream, the next day, I walked out to this left-hand area of the fence and the house and looked at it, and there's only a six-inch space/gap (at the most) between where the fence met the house. There was absolutely <u>no way</u> that he could get through that space. He weighed sixty pounds or more. I quickly dismissed the dream.

Lo and behold, a few days later I was putting some indoor plants outside while it was raining. I looked over and literally saw Eli go through that left-hand opening! He was actually a very skinny dog when he was soaking wet. All of that hair was deceiving because it was so fluffy. He was evidently spooked by the rain (even though he didn't bark at all), and he was slippery and able to get right through that space! God knew all along what was going on and He was trying to show me, but I just couldn't believe that it was true. God was giving me the **answer to the question that I had been asking** about how in the world Eli was getting out. This literal picture dream was the answer that we needed in order to remedy Eli's escape and keep him safe and contained.

Dream 2. Background Information First

One day a young lady from our church came to me in tears. She said that she had had a dream about me. Just so you know, she and I were just passing acquaintances at church. I didn't know her well at all nor did she know me well. She did not know that I was a regular dreamer, and I didn't know anything about her in regards to dreams either. She was sobbing, and she said that she had dreamed about me the night before.

The Car Accident Dream—She dreamed that I was in a horribly tragic car accident. She saw that I had lost the use of both legs and that I was in a wheelchair. End of dream.

I immediately felt that this dream was from the Lord and that it was a warning regarding the intentions of the enemy. At the time, I was the head of a women's and children's dance ministry. We had begun traveling and ministering in prisons and various community venues to further the gospel and bring people to Jesus. I prayed and asked the Lord for protection, but I felt that I was to be especially on the lookout when driving.

In real life here's what happened just a few days later, after she shared this dream with me:

My husband was driving, and I was in the passenger side of the car. We were going through a major intersection, and he was turning left. We had the green light right-of-way. As he started into the turn, I noticed that a car was coming toward the intersection in front of us and had the red light and should stop. Instead, this particular car actually started speeding faster and came through the intersection just as my husband was halfway into the turn. My husband was not aware of this and did not see the speeding car as he was looking in the direction that he was turning. I SCREAMED for him to "STOP!" and thankfully, he did…just as the car grazed us. The driver was speeding and did not even stop to see if we were all right. If my husband had gone any further into that turn, that car would have crashed right into my side of the vehicle at over sixty miles per hour. Needless to say, it would have been a very bad wreck. God gave me **a direct warning regarding trouble and the intentions of the enemy. I am still so thankful even to this day!** Just to note: The dance ministry that I was involved in grew in number and in further spreading the gospel for many, many years after that day. I ended up with a twenty-plus-member adult dance team and a wonderful dance school that ministered to hundreds of children of all ages teaching several forms of Christian dance. Eventually we offered large dance training conferences. The Lord really blessed this ministry, and I know that the enemy had plans to thwart it, but due to the obedience of this woman, his plans were stopped.

Literal Dreams about Friends and Family—I can't stress enough how important it is to recognize that most dreams are about/ for YOU. It is quite common to dream about other people that you know and think that the dream is about them; MOST of the time, though, the dream is really for or about YOU.

Occasionally, though, God will give you a dream that involves someone else and that is really FOR someone else. You have to be so very, very cautious in sharing these kinds of dreams because people aren't always as excited as you are (!) about hearing dreams about themselves. Also, in sharing dreams with others, we need to really have instruction from the Lord about it. Many times, He has given me a dream that I truly felt was about someone else, but I was given the dream for understanding and revelation on how to PRAY for that person, not in order to share the dream with them! It is an awesome responsibility to be trusted with these kinds of dreams, and I take it very seriously, and I believe that the Lord does as well. I strongly encourage you to PRAY earnestly before sharing dreams with others. Prayer may be the only thing that you are to do, if anything, with these dreams. Let's look at another biblical example to further illustrate:

Genesis 37 gives us some great insight about sharing dreams with others. The story is about an avid dreamer, Joseph. Joseph tells his brothers two dreams that he has had about them. Both dreams insinuate that they will be bowing down to him and giving him honor in some way. His brothers, the scriptures say, already hated him! So much so that they plotted to kill him calling him "this dreamer" in Genesis 37:19. They were already jealous of Joseph, but the dreams spurned their hatred further. Instead of killing him, they ended up throwing him in a pit. Then they sell him to travelers and tell their father, Jacob, that Joseph has been devoured by a ferocious animal, bringing to Jacob Joseph's coat which they have dipped with goat blood to make it look like he has been eaten.

This is horrendous! I might even go so far as to say that Joseph's sharing of the dreams inspired his brothers to perform these horrible acts. Can you imagine how it must have been for them to live with their father, Jacob, all of those years and knowing the truth about what happened to Joseph but hating him so MUCH that they never could even bring themselves to tell Jacob the truth? We know that God had a divine plan in all of it, but still, the sharing of dreams with others and the consequences that can bring is a solemn principle to take to heart.

So pray carefully before sharing dreams with others because not everyone takes them well. I am definitely a truth-seeker. Even when it is painful, I crave the truth, and I have a real problem with lies and people that tell them. But not everyone is this way, and not everyone wants to hear the truth! Here are two more literal dreams, and they both involve sharing dreams that are about others with the people in the dream:

Dream 3

The Shackled and in Concrete Dream—This dream involved a very close young friend that I knew. I dreamed that he kept getting in some kind of trouble but that he was getting away with it. I couldn't see in the dream exactly what the trouble was. He had been keeping this trouble hidden, but all of the sudden, a policeman bound him, and he was shackled and in concrete. He couldn't move, and his trouble was exposed for everyone to see. End of dream.

In real life, two days later, I was talking with the young man whom this dream was about, and I felt very strongly that I was to share the dream with him. I shared it with him, and he got very silent and really didn't say anything. I also told him that I felt that this was a **warning** dream and that God was trying to help him and was warning him in regards to whatever the "trouble" was that it would be exposed. **I believed that God was giving him the opportunity to deal with this before exposure took place.** Within ten days of dreaming the dream, it came to pass. This young man was arrested for drunk driving. The offense was pretty extreme, and it resulted in his having to pay three exorbitant fines (over eight thousand dollars) in lieu of serving time. He really was shackled and in concrete because it took him a long, long time (years) to pay the fines off, and he had to put off other things in his life until he completed the payoffs. Although he didn't really heed the warning, God was trying to help him. And this could have been prevented had he listened and taken the warning to heart. I so wished that he had listened. It was a hard lesson to learn, but the Lord truly was trying to help him. I didn't know what the "trouble" was, but I felt a prompting from the Lord to share this dream, and I had to leave the outcome with Him.

Dream 4

The Baby Boy Dream—I dreamed that some friends of ours were going to have another baby, and it was going to be a boy. End of dream.

Soon after having this dream, my husband and I were invited over to this lovely family's home for a meal. The family consisted of a husband and wife and four beautiful children (three girls and a boy). We were all seated and having a scrumptious meal. We were all enjoying the evening when I casually asked them if they were considering having another child. The wife became excited and wondered why I was asking. I felt that it was okay to share the dream, and I strongly felt that it was a literal dream (not symbolic), so I announced that they should "get ready" for another baby; a boy, as the dream entailed. The wife was happy about this "news," but the husband got pretty upset and asked us to leave! He was somewhat joking, but the truth is he <u>was</u> a little miffed and didn't really want to talk about it. I think that he felt that their quiver was full enough. We didn't talk much else about it that night. Needless to say, five months later, the wife announced that she was pregnant, and they did have a beautiful baby boy whom they named Paul. This family moved away, and to this day, I have not met Paul, but I recently spoke to the mom, and she describes him as "the most tender-hearted child and best hug-giver ever. He loves watching YouTube videos to figure out how things are made. He is 'all boy' and enjoys making wooden swords in the basement with his dad," she says. I hope to meet Paul one day soon! I feel honored that the Lord would include me in giving a message to this lovely family **about the future blessing that He had for them**.

I've had many more literal dreams, but hopefully, these are giving you an idea of the kinds of messages that God may relay through a literal dream for others. Remember to pray about them before sharing them with others as their response may or may not be pleasant. Unfortunately, you cannot make or force someone to listen to you or to take what you have to say seriously. All you can do is be a messenger (if that is what you are even supposed to do!) and trust God with the results.

One last thought about literal dreams. God is very personal. We cannot fathom how MUCH God loves us and how much He yearns for us to allow Him to be involved in our daily lives. He LONGS to help us, and He is so very practical. He knows everything about us: the good, the bad, and the ugly. He wants to HELP; I can't say that enough. All we have to do is invite Him. Ask Him. He is thrilled to take part.

Prepare yourself when you are praying over your dreams and be ready to realize that God is many times answering your requests in very practical ways. In other words, I HAVE to say it again: **don't over-spiritualize!** As Christians, we have a real tendency to do this, and, I feel, that we miss the boat when we are always trying to make things "mean something spiritual." Take, for instance, the "**Three-Plant Dream**" as a great example of the practicality of God in my life:

Dream 5

The Three-Plant Dream—Recently, I had a short, concise dream, and I saw three flowering plants that were dying at the edge of a road. I kept looking up and down the road, but I kept returning to the three plants and noticing that they were not far from being totally dead. End of dream.

After writing down this dream the next day, I immediately began to think of what these three plants could represent—friends, people, choices, etc.? For over a week, I went over the dream wondering what those "plants" were and what the "the edge of the road" could mean in my life. Finally, as I am literally turning into my driveway at the end of a day running errands, I see that my **"three plants"** by my mailbox, which is **"by the road,"** are dying. Over the past month, I had planted a lot of flowers all over the back and front yard. I had been tending to all of the freshly planted plants but especially the ones up close to the house. I had not given much attention to the ones that were out by the road because we have an underground sprinkler system that waters regularly in that area. I was surprised to see those three plants dying because I knew that the sprinkler system was covering them. But as it turns out, the zone that covers the edge of the road area was malfunctioning and was not spraying correctly. We did not know this because the sprinkler system runs on a timer quite early in the morning while we are still sleeping, so we just assumed that all of the zones were intact. It was totally missing those particular three plants! If I had taken the dream at face value (literally), I may have salvaged those plants, but too much time had gone by (with me spiritualizing the dream!), so I lost them. We were, however, able to rectify the malfunctioning zone and plant some other plants in that spot. Once again, God was showing me how very practical He is and how much He cares about the regular mundane things in my life.

To summarize: Literal dreams are straightforward in nature, and they speak to actual/factual things in your life or in the lives of those around you. They can be about ANYTHING, so keep an open mind when seeking the Lord as to your response to the dream.

Most often the purpose in a literal dream will be to give a warning, to give instruction, and/or to give revelation about the past, present, or for the future.

Take heed that you do not "spiritualize" your dreams. Remember that God is PRACTICAL and gives practical dreams for everyday life situations.

CHAPTER 5

SYMBOLISM TIPS AND FINDING THE MESSAGE

Be still and know that I am God.

—Psalm 46:10

I caution against using dream dictionaries to interpret symbols because as I keep reiterating: dreams are **personal** to the dreamer, and what may mean one thing to you may represent something totally different to another individual. Keeping this in mind, when you feel that the dream is not literal but is more symbolic in nature, it is important that you **personalize** the dream. What do I mean by personalize? Well, several things. It is important to look for the "key ingredient," the thing that stands out to you the most in the dream. Is it a person, a place, a color, an emotion? Is it an animal? After contemplating this key ingredient, then you should apply it personally to your life or situation. Let's look at some different aspects of symbolic dreams. I have right much to say about these, so be patient with me and with yourself as you take it all in.

Seeing yourself in the dream. I want to make three points about seeing yourself in the dream:

1. The dream could be just that. It could literally be about you, and you are to watch the dream just like a movie and see what you are doing in the dream and how it relates to your life and to what the Lord might be showing you.

51

2. Sometimes I am there (in the dream), but I am not a part of what is going on in the dream, necessarily. I could be watching or looking down on the dream as an observer, and I may experience emotions or thoughts or feelings about what I am seeing. I have found that the Lord, many times, uses these kinds of dreams to allow me to experience how HE sees the situation and what HE is saying about what is going on in the dream.

3. This last concept is a "new" one for me, but the Lord has spoken to me about this in the last year and has been showing me that sometimes I can dream about me and another person. Sometimes I will know the second person. But most of the time, I do not know them and have never met them. What He is showing me is ME...in two different ways. He is using the second person in the dream to show me things about myself that I may not recognize, and He also uses the second person to show me different things about myself that I might not see otherwise or might not *want* to see. It is more obvious when the second person is next to me in the dream because then I can compare my actions, thoughts, and reactions to this other person's.

It is always important to not just take it for granted when you are in a dream that the dream is about you. The dream may have a message for you (and most of the time it does!), but ask the Lord to show you, particularly, your place in the dream's meaning.

Now, let's look very generally at some common things in dreams and I will throw some thoughts out for you. People, places, animals, words, etc.—all of these are quite regular in dreams. The key is this: What does this thing represent to **you** personally?

PEOPLE—You can have a dream about yourself or a person that you know, and it can be a literal warning or piece of information about that person as we saw in the previous chapter. However, sometimes you can dream about a person in a dream, and that person is symbolic rather than literal. You then have to think of what that person means to *your* life. **And what that person represents or sym-**

bolizes to you is what the Lord is speaking to YOU about. Example: There is one woman that I dream of quite regularly. She is a wonderful and kind person, but she is extremely scatter-brained. When I dream of her, usually the Lord is speaking to <u>me</u> about organization or clarity, and He is encouraging me not to be scatter-brained but to seek Him for direction, guidance, and peace (or something along those lines) in regards to something that is presently going on in my life (remember to keep in mind that the dream is primarily for or about <u>you</u>).

Also, in regards to people in a dream, this is a little complicated, but sometimes in real life when I have been praying for someone, I may have a dream that is totally about that person, but in the dream a different person represents them. This has happened several times. Just recently, I had been asking the Lord for direction regarding another employee that we have been having problems with. This particular employee is extremely tall (in real life). I had a dream that gave me some answers about what to do with this employee, but in the dream, it wasn't him; instead, it was another extremely tall person (that I know) that reminds me of him. I am not sure why this happens except that I have wondered if the Lord does this in order to keep the focus more on the <u>message that He was giving me in the dream</u> rather than on the person in the dream. I have a tendency to dissect too much about the person in the dream (what they're wearing, doing, etc.) rather than focus on the <u>intent</u> of the message. This is intense, but if another person represents the real person, then I am totally thrown off track about analyzing the physical person, and I am able to focus more on **what God is trying to show me ABOUT the person's behavior, which is usually the heart of the matter.**

Lastly, in regards to people, you may dream about famous people. Again, just ask yourself what that person represents to **you**. Example: If I dreamed about Tom Selleck (what a hunky dream!), I would think a handsome man and a good communicator. I asked my husband what Tom Selleck represented to him, and he said, "A good person, someone with morals/values." I want you to see that he represents something totally different to my husband than to me. Just ask yourself the same question, and <u>be honest</u> about what that person truly represents to you and you will find that it will be helpful in the overall dream interpretation.

Sometimes, too, a person can represent a theme that the Lord is speaking to you about in the overall scope of the dream. If you are dreaming about a president, then the dream could revolve around something in hierarchy order in your life such as a boss or a teacher or pastor or someone that makes decisions in some kind of way (over you) or even yourself (!) in these regards. You may dream about a famous business person or a famous artist and, after prayer, realize that the dream revolves around your own work/business situation or around creativity in your life in some way.

ANIMALS/REPTILES/INSECTS—Many times the generic traits of an animal are what they represent in a dream. Snakes can represent lies or deception. Bulls can represent sacrifice or even being a "klutz" like bull-in-a-china-shop. A dog or cat could represent something that you love and care for or a nuisance, depending on how you feel personally about this pet. Alligators can represent a powerful bite which could relate to verbal trouble—gossip, snapping at people, etc. Spiders like to weave webs that you can get caught up in and can "spin" tales and cause trouble.

PLACES—Places can be very personal. Many times, you will see or be in a place in your dream. It is important to note where that is. The "scene" of the dream. Is it a place from your past, present, or a place that you want to be in the future? Is it a place you've never been to? Is this a real or imaginary place? Is this a symbolic place? Answering these questions will help to get to the message in the dream.

Now I would like to share a dream and its interpretation regarding a symbolic place, but I have to give you some background information so that you will understand it:

Background Information First: My husband, Dennis, was in love. He had poured himself and much of his money (!) into a four-wheel rust bucket (the love of his life), a 1976 Ford F150 long bed truck that he had acquired for five hundred dollars. He spent hours with this truck; sanding and painting it, putting custom wheels and tires on it, replacing doors, and lots of other parts. It was his pride and joy. He was bringing it back to life, and it gave him a great hobby. One morning, we awoke early and had to run some much-needed errands. We opened the front door and realized that the truck was gone. Stolen! It was stolen out of our own front yard. Dennis was furious! So was I. We called the police. We filed a report. They said they would be on the lookout for it but that most likely the thief would paint it quickly so it wouldn't be recognized since it was a very bright red-and-white, two-tone color. I begged the Lord to return it to us. Within days of the theft, I had the following dream:

The Red and White Truck Dream—I had a picture dream. (Remember the definition of a picture dream from the first dream mentioned earlier in the previous chapter? A picture dream is like a photograph.) Here it is:

In the dream, I saw the truck! It was parked across town in a location where a popular Steak and Ale restaurant used to be. This restaurant sat in a corner of a shopping center near the road, and it was uniquely angled where two crossroads came together, and it sat caddy cornered. The truck was parked there, but it was facing (pointed toward) a road across the street which was the interstate. The only other thing that stood out to me in the dream was that everything was at an angle. In other words, the picture dream was not square or rectangle like a normal picture would be. Instead, it was more on a diagonal and angled just like the true location of the restaurant was. End of dream.

OUTCOME OF DREAM: When I woke up the next morning, the picture image of the truck in that location encouraged me so much. I was so certain that the truck would be there that the next day I woke up and wrote it down and then I literally drove to that abandoned restaurant across town and was sure I would see it. (Here goes the literal part again; remember that I said our first inclination is to interpret dreams literally?). I arrived at the location. The building was still standing there but at the time was not inhabited by anyone. It still had the old "Steak and Ale" sign up. I looked across the street in the direction that the truck was facing in the dream only to see the interstate and cars whizzing by. Frustrated and confused, I went home. I reread and reread the dream and kept asking the Lord to show me more. After a couple of days, I started thinking about "any" steak restaurant that might still be in operation that I knew of that was shaped like that because it had such a unique shape to it and a unique caddy corner location. What I kept coming back to was the **angle/shape** of the dream and the location being shaped that way. I couldn't think of a steak restaurant, but there was a very popular Fish House restaurant in another section of town, and it wasn't too far from our home, and it was shaped very similar to the restaurant in the dream. In fact, it was the ONLY restaurant that I could think of that had THAT KIND OF SHAPE. I became a little frightened. Did I dare go to it? I had never been to this restaurant before, and it was in a sketchy area that was known for crime. What was I going to do? Was I going to go in there and ask if anyone had seen our truck? I HAD to go. My curiosity was too great.

I drove to the Fish House restaurant. Yes, it was shaped a lot like the restaurant in my dream, and it was located in a crossroads and sat caddy corner just like in my dream. I looked in the parking lot and did not see the truck. But then I looked in the direction where the truck was pointing in my dream and there was a road. I had never been down this road before. It was in an area known for crime. I started down the road, praying as I went and asking the Lord to guide me and keep me safe. (If my husband had known where I was, HE would have killed me.) I passed about four houses and then noticed a group of guys behind a house and standing beside a garage. Behind the group of guys in the shadows was **our truck!** I could not believe it! I get chills to this day thinking about it. I immediately called my husband, and I also called the police. I wanted to bust up in there and tell them all that they weren't so clever and that God had given us our truck back, but instead, I obeyed the police who told me to ride around the block until they could get there to apprehend the criminals. When the police arrived, the group scattered, and the cops didn't even want to go into the area that they were in because according to them, it was an area known for extreme violence. But they did, and we retrieved our truck. The thieves had started sanding it in order to paint it another color. Also, they had used a screwdriver to steal it by busting out the ignition, which is incidentally what we had to use to start it in order to drive it back home. Hallelujah! That dream was from the Lord, and to this day, I still thank Him for it and for speaking to me through dreams!

Hopefully, by now you are considering the different aspects of your own dream language. It is at this time that I would like to interject a KEY element—RESPONSE. What is response? Response is something that is done as a reaction to something else. If you want to grow from your dream experiences, you <u>have</u> to respond! You have to take action. And many times, you have to take a chance. Being just an observer of the dream will not get you the desired results. When I was driving to the Fish House restaurant, I felt a "little crazy." I really wasn't expecting to necessarily find the truck, but I was hoping for some kind of clue or confirmation of something more. All I was really doing was responding to the only other thing that I could think of that the dream reminded me of. But that is the point: I <u>was</u> responding. And praise God (!); I got it! I got the answer, the truck, the interpretation—everything! I wasn't crazy, after all! God <u>did</u> give me that dream. You will never know until you try; just follow the inclination that you are having. You have to follow through with a response. Seek and you <u>shall</u> find. But you have to seek; you have to take the risk of being wrong in order to learn and improve in discerning and in interpreting your dreams. This is a basic principle of spiritual obedience.

Of course, finding our truck through a dream was a major eye-opener for me in regards to the importance of dreams. It gave me a renewed confidence to move forward in this area. I am hoping that you are gaining confidence as you read this in regards to your own personal dream language and that you will have the courage to respond to your dream, in some way, if you need to.

As we continue to look at symbolic dreams, I want to stress an important point to you. It is easy to get real caught up on the symbolism part of the dream, so much so that you can actually start getting confused and off track and miss the real intent of the dream, which is always the **message**. So let's look at some more symbolic dreams with a focus on finding the message.

Finding the Message in Symbolic Dreams

Some dreams can be crazy. Yes, I mean it. They can be VERY strange. But I encourage you to try not to immediately discard them because there truly are some of the best messages hidden within really weirdo dreams, so try not to focus on the weirdness but rather on the message and the intent of the dream. I mean, truly, this is a real key in all of dream interpretation; you have to get past the weird element and not get hung up on trying to make it all make sense because it just won't make sense (to your mind) most of the time. BUT if you dig a little deeper and try looking at the central theme of the dream, this is where you can usually find the MESSAGE. I am going to share some more personal dreams with you to further illustrate this and how it works, so dig in with your own "message shovel" and watch for the intent in each dream:

Blocked Asphalt Dream—In the dream, I had parked my car in a downtown area, and I had gotten out to walk around. I was headed in a certain direction, but then I was blocked from continuing forward. I couldn't continue walking due to these construction workers who were repaving the asphalt. I tried to walk around them in another direction as I was trying to get back to my car, and my way became even worse. It appeared that the asphalt work was growing and spreading all on its own. I felt panicked and then it was like I was completely blocked in and I not only couldn't get back to my car, but I couldn't get out at all. I was screaming and yelling for help at the construction workers, but they couldn't hear me at all due to all of the construction noise, and they weren't paying any attention to me either, and they really didn't seem to care anyway. Then I grabbed some kind of overhead pulley system, and I just figured that I was so stuck that it was my only way out, and I was able to hold onto it and ride it down out of the asphalt area like a zip line, and I was free. End of dream.

What I felt that the message was: *There is a growing problem, and I am trying to move forward in some way, but I can't. Neither I nor anyone else can help me. The problem may remain, but it looks like God will provide a way for me to go over it.*

Ready for the interpretation?

In real life, Dennis and I were trying to sell a house. We had many people show strong interest in the home; however, they were constantly getting hung up over a private road (asphalt!) that led to the house and the fact that there was no formal maintenance agreement drawn up for this road. (Note: the asphalt part of the dream and how I was constantly getting blocked in by it and it was a growing problem!) I truly felt that there was an answer inside of this dream for our dilemma. I thought and prayed about this for a couple of days, and in the meantime, the road maintenance problem kept coming up even more! My husband and I decided that we would have to take measures into our own hands, and we set out to have a road maintenance agreement drawn up by an attorney and then to convince our neighbors to sign this form. All along I felt like, in the end, that we would be okay without a road maintenance agreement and that there would come along a buyer who would buy the house regardless (just like in the dream where I zip-lined out of the situation) and we would be scot-free of the problem. But the form seemed necessary, and we knew from our agent that certain banks wouldn't loan money without the form in place. Long story short, we never could get one of the neighbors to sign the form. But a buyer did come along who wasn't concerned about the road, and his bank wasn't concerned about it either! He did request to have a copy of the form (unsigned) for his records though, and he was quite satisfied with that. So in reality, we DID go scot-free just like the zip line, and we were able to close the deal and dodge the whole asphalt (private road) situation, but it was important to the buyer in the overall sale of the home that we had made the effort to deal with this problem, and if I hadn't had the dream, I don't think that we would have even tried.

I will have to say that this dream carried me through several weeks of agony, and I even told our real estate agent about it and the fact that I felt like in the end we would "zip line" out of the situation. She watched it take place and was so pleasantly surprised! I am so thankful for the Lord's care to reveal the problem but also to reveal that there would be a successful outcome.

NOTE: If I had focused on the craziness of the dream's details such as being downtown, or stuck, or riding a zip line out of nowhere, or seeing asphalt spreading, then I would have totally missed the **message** in the dream that was being given to help me in my daily life situation.

Let's look at more crazy dreams and their messages.

Before telling you this next dream, I want to share something personal that coincides with the dream. In real life and at the time of the dream, I was going to a Christian counselor for some emotional issues from my past that kept surfacing. I really didn't know what else to do with these things, and I knew that I needed to talk with someone as these things were from my childhood, but they just would not go away.

Here is the dream that I had during this time:

The Beatles' Song Dream—In the dream, I saw a 45 record, and it had a long scratch going all the way across the vinyl. The song was "She Loves You" by the Beatles. In the dream, I hoped that the scratch wouldn't affect the song, but I knew that it HAD to affect the playing of the song since it went all the way across the vinyl. End of dream.

When I woke up, I asked the Lord if this could be about me and my ability to love or receive love. In real life, I did not associate the emotional issues that I was having with the ability to love, but after going through the counseling, it was quite obvious that the "scratch" of the issues did go all the way through my life and loving relationships and that it had affected me deeply and those I tried to love. Having this dream helped me to recognize this, accept and deal with these struggles. I received healing in these areas over time, but the dream helped prepare me to face the deep hurts and wounds.

NOTE: It would have been easy to toss this dream out thinking it was silly due to it being about a record and the Beatles, etc., but I had to choose to focus on the central part of the dream, which was where the message was.

The Importance of Similarities

Recognize similarities in your dreams. I emphasize the word SIMILARITIES. Remember the red-and-white truck dream? Remember how the restaurant in the dream was so very similar to the restaurant that I drove to when I found the truck? That was a key element in interpreting that dream for me.

What do I mean by similarities? Look for things in the dream that are very similar to things that are going on in your life. This helps in getting to the message. When you wake up, what stands out **the most** to you in the dream? As I have said before, after praying, go back to the dream and underline key things. Then write a short summary of what you feel the dream is speaking to you about and/or the message, taking note of "similarities" in your life.

I am going to now present a dream that I had recently, and we are going to go through it step-by-step and find the message together:

The Pool Shooter Dream—In the dream, I was being asked to help a younger woman and teach her how to shoot pool. She was very serious about it and was practicing her skills at home. We were going to go to a pool hall and practice on a table there. When we got there, I was looking for a good table. I asked someone in charge about a tournament table (regulation size) that we could practice on, and they said it was "in the back" and it was folded up and could not be used right now. I really wanted her to shoot on a regulation size table, but since it wasn't available, we looked at the tables that were available. They were smaller and narrower, and they just weren't right. I didn't want her to practice on any of those because I knew that they were the wrong size, and I didn't want her to learn incorrectly. The dream ended with us just looking at the wrong tables. They just weren't what she needed.

Here are the words that I went back and underlined that stood out to me in the dream. Here it is again:

> In the dream, I was being asked to <u>help a younger woman and teach her how to shoot pool.</u> <u>She was very serious about it and was practicing her skills at home</u>. We were going to go to a pool hall and practice on a table there. When we got there, I was <u>looking for a good table</u>. I asked someone in charge about a tour-

nament table (regulation size) that we could practice on, and they said it was "in the back" and it was folded up and <u>could not be used right now</u>. I really wanted her to shoot on a regulation size, but since it wasn't available, we looked at the tables that were available. They were smaller and narrower, and they just weren't right. I didn't want her to practice on any of those because I knew that they were the wrong size, and I didn't want her to learn incorrectly. The dream ended with us just looking at the wrong tables. <u>They just weren't what she needed</u>.

What I felt that the message was: *There is someone (most likely a younger girl or woman) less experienced than me that is looking to me for help. I am trying to help her, but the timing is not right yet and/or the situation is not right.*

Also, this dream immediately reminded me of someone in my life and of present similarities. Even though I did not recognize the woman in the dream, the overall dream reminded me so much of my niece, Cierra.

Now let me give you some background information: In real life, I am pretty decent in shooting pool. We owned a pool table for several years, and my husband and I actually met shooting pool. I have also shot in a couple of tournaments. So basically, this dream spoke to me about teaching someone less experienced about a skill that I possess. I have to interject here that the dream reminded me of (is SIMILAR to) something myself and my oldest niece, Cierra, were recently discussing. At the time, she and I were talking about the possibility of her going into business for herself. I have had several businesses, and she has never had a business, so the dream immediately made me think of her and her situation. She was even talking about looking for a location to have this business in. As in the dream, we were looking for a good table, but it just wasn't available right now. The ones that were available were just not what she needed. I remember when I woke up from the dream, I thought that we just needed to wait because the timing just wasn't right due to the "right table" not being available.

Cierra had recently talked to me about her business ideas and asked me about them. I had been asking the Lord to show me/us about this, and after having this dream, I just felt like He was telling me that the timing wasn't right yet and that I needed to just wait rather than offer her more advice. I resisted the urge to talk with her about it the next time we got together, and shortly after having this dream, she accepted a job in our hometown that would help develop her skills even further in the area of business that she is seeking to be in. She is "practicing her skills at home," just as the dream said, and, hopefully, in the future when the time is right and everything is ready, she will be able to move forward with her business ideas, and I may be able to help her more then.

This may seem like a simple analogy, but this is a great example of how to decipher and find the message in the dream. In this case, it was very similar to things that were going on in my life. I encourage you to look for _similarities_ when you are interpreting.

God is very patient with us. He is willing to invest endless amounts of time into teaching us lessons in life. He knows our frustrations, and He is more than willing to help us and encourage us. There are many dreams that I have had that I feel could have meaning but I just cannot interpret. Also, there have been many that just mean absolutely nothing to me. In addition, there are seasons where I just don't dream much at all.

I believe that just as there are natural seasons (spring, summer, fall, and winter), there are spiritual seasons that we go through. It is in the "going through" these times and experiencing changes in life where we really learn to hone in on hearing and recognizing God's voice. To further expound, when you hear someone talk all of the time, it can be really easy not to listen because you just get tired of all of the chatter and endless words. But then when you are with someone who doesn't talk much and they then open their mouth to speak, you become more interested in listening, really **listening** to what they have to say. So it is with God.

In a spiritual "winter," dreams may die down making your dream life very quiet. It is important that you continue to write down and acknowledge any dream that you do have during these times because you can be sure that the Lord is still teaching you even in His silence. It was during one of these quieter dream seasons that I experienced a marvelous unveiling of God's faithfulness, and BELIEVE IT OR NOT, another vehicle was stolen!

This time, it was from our business. It was almost as if God was letting me know that He was well able to do it *again*. I really didn't want to have to be taught this lesson, but if I am really, truly honest with you, I can say that it was necessary. Why? Well, to be totally honest, because I was still struggling with the whole dream validity thing. I know. It's hard to admit, but it is true. Even after all of the answers to prayers and confirmations and life-changing things that had already happened up to this point, I was still questioning the Lord about dreams and their **really** being from Him. So this time, He gave the dream to my husband. Here is the real-life "setup" for what transpired:

One evening at around ten o'clock, Dennis and I both fell asleep in our living room while watching TV. The phone rang and startled us out of our slumber. It was one of our employees, and he was hysterically yelling that someone came into his yard and stole his (our) work van! (Note: Our employees drive the work vans to their homes). My first thought was that he was drunk, but he wasn't. I frantically relayed this information to Dennis, and he said, "That's funny, I was just now dreaming about one of our vans. The phone woke me up from the dream." I hung the phone up, telling our employee that we were coming right over. Then I asked my husband to tell me everything that he remembered about the dream that he was having. Here it is:

The Stolen Van Dream—In the dream, Dennis saw one of our plumbing vans being driven recklessly. The van was being driven wildly through people's yards. He could not see the driver. In the next scene, my husband was walking in a building, and he saw an old man who told him that what he was looking for would be on top of a hill. End of dream.

Since this had just happened, we grabbed our keys and ran to our car and headed toward the employee's home to investigate as fast as possible. We hoped to possibly pass the thief along the way as it was a long drive to the home of our employee. As we were driving, I told my husband that the only thing that was coming to me about his dream was there is an area of town in our city known as "Fort Hill." It is the only "hill" that I could think of, and the "hill" comment in the dream was what stood out more than anything else.

We drove to the employee's home. He explained that he was actually trying to start his personal car by hooking up the work van with cables (jump-start). So he had the work van running, and a man walked up and suddenly opened the van door and jumped in and stole it. The man drove recklessly through the neighborhood as he tried to get away as fast as possible. We could see the turned over trash cans and debris, etc. in the neighborhood that the thief's reckless driving caused, and my husband said that is what he saw in his dream.

I was insistent that we drive to the Fort Hill area of town to investigate. This area was nowhere close to where we were, but it was the only "hill" that I could think of. Dennis agreed, and the employee who had joined us in our car was confused, so we relayed the information about the dream, etc., as we drove to Fort Hill.

We turned onto the first road in the Fort Hill area and went about one-fourth mile, and as we were in a curve, we noticed woods to our left and there it was! Our stolen van! The thief was in the process of unloading equipment out of the van and carrying it through the woods to his destination. We caught him right in the act. He ran off. We stayed and called the police to file a report. HALLELUJAH! Once again, the Lord proved Himself mighty to save and had given us the location of the stolen van earlier in Dennis's dream even BEFORE the van actually arrived there! Well, you can believe that any skepticism that I had was quickly vanishing; it is a humbling experience but well worth it to be taught lessons from the Lord. He is so very patient, and I so appreciate His willingness to work with me and grow my faith!

As you can see, the **message** was obvious. What we could have done in this situation was treat the dream as if it was just a coincidence. We could have also dismissed the "hill" part of the dream, which would have been also quite unfortunate because this was the KEY. I hope this helps you, especially with the "similarities" part of this chapter. This happens many times to me, having dreams that are very similar to something in my life, and I have learned over time to really pay attention to this and compare the dreams' contents to the similar things in my life, applying them when I feel instructed to after prayer and seeking the Lord.

This chapter has been devoted to going over some symbolism tips for you. We will look at some further symbolic topics as we continue, but I want to give you one more thing to consider before concluding this chapter.

As much as we would like for dream interpretation to be "cut and dry," the real truth is that it just plain isn't. It requires prayer and seeking the Lord for answers and confirmation. The previous chapter was on literal dreams, and this chapter on symbolism, but you should also know that dreams can have a little of BOTH. I would be misleading you by not telling you this, and it muddies the waters and makes it a little messy, but it is the truth. So how can I conclude this chapter on symbolism? Be open. Be flexible. Keep in mind that most times it is primarily either literal or symbolic, but it can have a little of both aspects. Try not to get frustrated but be patient in this journey. You will grow in understanding and recognizing these differences.

To summarize: Symbolism dreams can be tricky to interpret. Watch for the "key ingredient." Remember to look for what the symbol (person, place, thing, emotion, etc.) could represent to you *personally.*

Some dreams require you to respond. They require you to step out, much like as you step out in faith. In order to grow and learn, you have to respond. You will make mistakes, but this is part of growth.

Do not get thrown off track by crazy or seemingly weird dreams. Continue seeking the **message. God uses weird things in order to get our attention!**

Similarities are very common and important. Dreams may not be exact, that is "word for word" (exactly) like what is in your life, but *pay attention* <u>to what the dream makes you think of or reminds you of, aka, the **similarity**</u>.

We will come back to symbolism and even "delicate" dreams ahead, but the next chapter is important. It is one that the Lord keeps encouraging me to include. Read it carefully and prayerfully.

CHAPTER 6

GOD STILL SPEAKS—SCRIPTURE, THE RHEMA WORD, AND THE HOLY SPIRIT

If you continue in my word, then you are
my disciples indeed; and you shall know the
truth and the truth shall make you free.
—John 8:31–32

And you shall seek me, and find me, when
you shall search for me with all your heart.
—Jeremiah 29:13

It is actually quite simple. So why do we make it so hard? What am I referring to? Reading the Bible. The "thees" and "thous" thrown in do make it a little weird, but if this bothers you, there are so many great versions that you can use rather than the King James Version. When I first became a Christian, I used the Living Bible along with the King James Bible. I would read passages in the Living Bible and then I would compare them to the same passages in the King James. This helped me **understand**. I knew that I needed understanding more than anything because I just didn't understand the Bible and that was an issue.

I can tell you after walking with Christ for almost forty years the Bible is the BEST resource for getting to know Him. Yes, you need ALL of it. By ALL of it, I mean prayer, going to church, Christian fellowship, worship, etc., but for me, I have found that I have come to KNOW HIM most and best by reading His Word. PERIOD. If you do not have a daily, or at least, very regular, quiet time that you set aside for Him in order to read the Bible and take in His Word, you are (spiritually) malnourished. And you can go to the best church in the world and do all of the right Christian things and volunteer for this and that, but you will be lacking majorly without feeding from His Word. John 1:1 tells us that the Word was in the beginning, and the Word was with God, and the Word was God. John 1:14 goes on to say that the Word was made flesh and dwelt among us. JESUS. He IS the Word. We have to feast upon Him, taking Him in daily for life-giving strength, guidance, and growth. It is so much more than reading. It is LIFE when we take in the Word. So my challenge to you if you aren't already doing so is to make it a requirement in your life; a requirement that you absolutely do not go without or put off. Read the Bible, praying over its words and asking for understanding as if it is your life jacket in the middle of the ocean because it is; it truly is.

On top of the spiritual strength and understanding about God that you will gain, you will also experience a closeness with the Lord like none other. You will find direction for your life, and you will find purpose. You will also recognize the Lord speaking directly to YOU, and you will joyfully embrace how real He really is in your life and how much He loves being included in every detail of your life. I want to share with you how I first experienced this great love and closeness.

I struggled growing up. I guess we all have struggled in some form or fashion. It's just a part of life. My struggles were mostly internal because I have always had a tendency to not let anyone know my inner feelings and inadequacies. I would compare myself to other kids my age, and I always felt "less than." On the positive side, I was pretty good at sports, and I had a competitive nature, so I threw myself into tennis, volleyball, softball, track and field, etc. These activities kept me away from harmful behavior for a good while, but eventually I began experimenting with drugs and alcohol.

Coupled with the fact that my dad got a job transfer while I was in high school AND that my parents were at the start of a divorce, my "free for all" lifestyle was spiraling downward fast. I struck out on my own and left home at the young age of sixteen, determined not to move to a strange place with them. As you can expect, this broke my parents' hearts. There really wasn't much that they could do with me because I was pretty stubborn and independent and had firmly decided to go my own way wherever that was.

Two horrible years later, after hitchhiking across the country, spending time in jail, and literally having near-death experiences, GOD got my attention. (Just so you know, I had a godly mother who had been praying for me during this time, and she also had every prayer group known to man praying. I would watch her relationship with the Lord and feverishly question everything about it. My mind-set at the time was that I just couldn't believe that a loving God could let horrible things happen in the world nor could He allow my family to go through a painful divorce and move, so basically, I didn't want to have anything to do with "Him" if "He" even existed.)

Thankfully, God saw through my bleeding, confused heart. He lovingly rescued me (and all of this is truly for another book, maybe, one day), but during my beginning, initial time of recognizing His reality, I opened one of my mom's devotional books and turned to a page that had this chapter's scripture on it (Jer. 29:13): "And you shall seek Me, and find Me, when you shall search for Me with **all your heart**." When I read this, it was as if the words jumped off the page. I honestly felt that God was speaking to me. Yes, little ole me! This was my first encounter with God actually "speaking" to me. I knew that He was saying this to me right then at that very moment and that He was looking for me to respond. No one had to tell me this. I just *knew* it.

This was a unique experience for me because when I was ten years old, I had accepted Jesus as my Savior, and I had tried reading the Bible, but I didn't understand most of what I was reading. This current experience, however, was different from just "reading."

This was more like communication. I found out as I grew in my Christianity after the Jeremiah 29:13 scripture jumped-off-the-page-and-God-spoke-to-me day (!) that this is a REAL thing. It's called a **rhema** word. The simple definition is that it is a direct specific word to a specific person in a specific situation. Why am I going into all of this? Because it is vitally important that we realize that

1. God is the interpreter of dreams, and
2. He will confirm the interpretation. He can confirm in many ways. It is always helpful to go to the Bible as you seek the Lord. Ask Him to give you a rhema word, a "now" word for your dream interpretation. At the very least, ask Him to give you scripture that will help clarify your dream if you need clarification.

I have experienced a rhema word in scripture many times since that first time, but I want to give you an illustration of this use of the rhema word in my own dream interpretation experience. I have also experienced times where I asked God for a rhema word and He did **not** give me one. It is important that we are willing to receive from Him in truth and not try and "make something" happen or make the outcome of a dream be something that it is not. This next illustration is kind of long, but please be patient until the end.

Illustration of a dream interpretation and a rhema word: *Background information first.* My husband and I had a business in North Carolina that we needed to sell. Because of the nature of this business, and because of the small town that it was in, we did not feel that we could advertise our need to sell it. We had to keep it private. So how were we to sell it? We began praying about it, and I had the following dream:

Antique Picture Dream—I had a picture dream. It was a strong and vivid picture of a decoration that you would see over antique doors or doorways or even fireplaces. It is called a "bull's-eye." (I didn't know the name of it then, but I found this out later). During the dream, I just recognized it from shopping in antique stores. End of dream.

Interpretation and message of the dream: When I woke up the next day, I just knew that this dream had something to do with the selling of our business. How did I know this? I just knew. It was a very strong picture dream, and I could not get the image out of my mind. I asked the Lord about it, and He said, "What does this remind you of?"

I said, "It reminds me of what I would see over an antique doorway or fireplace."

He then said, "And what does **that** remind you of?"

The ONLY thing I could think of was that there are several antique shops in our North Carolina town, but there is only ONE of them that stands out to me. It is run by a lady named Judy that I have spoken to a couple of times. So I asked the Lord if He was encouraging me to go and speak with her about our need to sell our business. (Note: She would not ever be someone that I would seek out to speak to because I really didn't know her very well and I could not be sure that I should trust her with this information. Also, there was a lot of business competition in this town, and if she wanted to, she could actually do more harm than good with this information. But I strongly felt that the Lord was encouraging me to go and tell her about our desire to sell.)

Antique picture dream's results: After confirming that it was okay with my husband, I set out the following day to speak with her. I arrived at her store, and it was closed. This could have discouraged me, but I just told the Lord if He wanted me to do this, then He was going to have to work out the details where she would be there and no one else would be around. I didn't get the opportunity to go back for several days, but when I did, she was there, and no one else was in the store. Nervously, I approached her and told her that I wanted to speak with her about something but that she would have to give me her word that this would be a confidential talk. She agreed, and I felt God's peace to continue. I told her the dream, and I told her that I felt that God was leading me to speak with her. I told her that we wanted to sell our business but that we didn't want anyone knowing this, and I wondered if she might be interested in buying it, or did she possibly know someone that might be interested? She got kind of quiet and then she said that she might know someone but that she didn't think she should bring it up to them. She said that she would wait until the next time they were together (as they occasionally went out for a meal to catch up on their lives) and she would bring it up **if** she felt comfortable that **they** would keep it quiet. I said, "Okay," thanked her, and left.

I was BEYOND disappointed. I was wholeheartedly expecting her to make me an offer on the spot or say that "she knew just the person." She assured me that she wouldn't tell anyone, but how could I be sure? I was discouraged and wondering if I had done the right thing. **Pause for an important tip.**

IMPORTANT TIP: It is at this point in your own dream interpretation when you can get the most frustrated and want to quit. When you feel sure that God has led you or that He has spoken to you and then the results are not what you expect, it can be VERY disheartening. But isn't this principle true in the majority of our Christian lives? Somehow, we think that things are going to be a certain way, and when they don't turn out that way, we have to decide if we are going to TRUST the Lord NO MATTER WHAT. Actually, He wants our implicit trust from the very beginning! If only we could just throw all those "expectations" out and trust that He knows what He is doing. It sure would save us a lot of grief!

Antique picture dream results continued: About three weeks later, the phone rang, and it was Judy. She had never called me on the phone. She was breathlessly excited! She did have dinner with those friends of hers who were a local couple, whom we did not know. In the midst of their dinner conversation, they told her that "They were ready for something new." She felt immediately that she needed to tell them about our store being for sale. She said that they were so excited! She gave them my phone number, and she expected them to call me at any moment. Within that hour, the wife called. She told me that she and her husband were extremely interested in finding out more, and she asked if she could meet with me that day.

We met, and long story short, they made a full price offer on our business! My husband and I were ecstatic! We had enlisted the help of a broker. The offer was contingent upon their being able to get financing. So get this: they could NOT get financing. But they were extremely interested and wanted to pay one-third down at the closing and then pay the other two-thirds over the next two years.

Okay, just so you know this about me. I have an accounting and finance background. I was pretty adamant (so was my husband) that we would not offer ANY financing. After all, we aren't a bank! We were trying to sell this business and be done with it, NOT prolong the agony of it. We were at a true rock and a hard place. See that last **IMPORTANT TIP**? The Lord was really dealing with us about trust. Trusting in Him. We were struggling though, because we knew that the dream was from Him, but this whole financing bit was not comfortable at all, and we did not have complete peace. SHOULD we go the financing route and finance over two years with these people? What if they destroyed the business? What if they didn't follow through and pay? Were we just to hand over our hard-earned business to them and trust their word?

The Rhema Word—One night in the midst of this turmoil, I was reading my Bible. I was just randomly reading, and this scripture jumped off the page. That is not a very good description. It didn't REALLY jump off the page, but the best way I can describe this is that the scripture just spoke directly to my heart at that very moment. It was like it was pertinent for ME in my life right THEN as opposed to reading it as history or as something to learn or study by. The scripture was Isaiah 14:24, "The Lord of hosts has sworn, saying, Surely as I have thought, so shall it come to pass; and as I have purposed, so shall it stand." A beautiful Rhema word just for our situation.

I was feeling that the Lord was saying that He is behind all of this with the financing and that He would see this through to the end and that we needed to trust HIM. I was still struggling even after receiving this special Rhema word, so a couple of days later, this SAME scripture appeared in my devotional for the morning. THERE IT IS AGAIN! Isaiah 14:24 (again!). Now, I REALLY KNEW that He was confirming that He would bring their financing to pass and that we were to move forward with the deal. My husband agreed. So we did. We agreed to the financing. We had the broker write up conditions in the contract just in case they reneged on the payments. But the outcome was as the Lord has said. The couple kept their word and paid us every month for the full two years just as promised. They kept their promise, but even more importantly, the Lord kept His promise.

You see, He had instigated this entire thing. From the dream to the financing to the finish. My only duty was to TRUST HIM.

I hope that you can see the use of a Rhema word from the Lord to help aid in your dream interpretation and in your life in general. The bottom line is that God confirms His will to us in many different myriads of ways. Scripture (period!) is one key way of confirmation and, particularly, the Rhema word for help with the situation.

One last thing I need to say about the Rhema word. If the interpretation of your dream does not line up with scripture, take a giant step back! Something is amiss. Allow the Lord to make everything plain and peaceable. He will not go against His Word, and as 1 Corinthians 14:33 says, "He is not the author of confusion, but of peace."

The Holy Spirit

As I contemplate my salvation experience, I can honestly say that way back when, in my ten-year-old mind, I had done everything that I knew to become a Christian. I had confessed and repented of my sins. I had accepted Jesus as my Savior. I professed Him, and I was reading my Bible. I hadn't been told about the importance of water baptism, and I certainly hadn't had anyone talk to me about the Holy Spirit. I knew that there was a Holy Spirit, and I believed in whatever it/He was, but I didn't understand it nor had I ever experienced anything with the Holy Spirit that I was aware of. But this was soon to change...especially for my mom.

In the neighborhood where I grew up, there were a couple of women who went to a Bible study, and they invited my mom to come. When she went, she found out that one of the other mothers had a son who was addicted to drugs. This mother asked for prayer, and all of the women in the Bible study decided to fast and pray for this son including my mom. While at home alone, where my mom was praying and fasting, she had a vision and saw Jesus come into our living room. It was during this experience that she received the baptism in the Holy Spirit. She also received a prayer language with tongues. I didn't know what any of this stuff meant. It was all like Greek to me.

This caused quite a ripple in our family. We actually thought that she had a mental problem there for a while because all she wanted to talk about was Jesus, and she even said that God spoke to her on a regular basis. The next couple of years were brutal because a real spiritual battle was taking place in our family, but I watched her, and I really saw a difference in her life. She had a beautiful peace and even a glow in her countenance. She was much more compassionate than she had ever been, and she prayed for each of us (and others) on a regular basis. She even began telling us things that God had told her and things that were going to happen, and they actually started happening! She started showing up for some of my athletic activities, which she had never really attended before. She was really trying to obey God and live according to what was in the Bible. Internally, I wondered if some of this God stuff was for real. Yet at sixteen, when I began living a "wild" life which included partying, stealing, drugs, alcohol, leaving home, etc., I wasn't convinced that there was more of God that **I** could experience. I mean, after all, God hadn't given ME that extra God stuff that He had given to my mom, so maybe I wasn't able to experience Him in any extra special way. I just didn't understand it all, and I was hurt and confused and rebellious and, frankly a little jealous. Also, I was angry because this change in my mom did not fare too well in my parents' relationship.

My struggles weren't too big for the Lord though, nor my mom because she continued to pray, and the Lord answered. When He did get my attention and I totally surrendered my life to Christ a few years later, I was sure that there had to be MORE. More than just reading my Bible. More than just going to church. After all, God was alive, not dead. Surely, He wanted more interaction, and He had evidently put it in my heart to want MORE of Him. My question over and over was how do I experience more of God?

So I began asking everyone this question. I asked God. I asked people at church. I asked my mom. And over and over I kept receiving the same answer. You need the baptism in the Holy Spirit. What, in the world, were they talking about? I just didn't understand it. Didn't I have the Holy Spirit already? When I would read scriptures in the Bible about the Holy Spirit, I was intrigued. What I saw when I read the Bible was that Jesus made a very big deal about the promise of the Holy Spirit. In John 14:16, He called the Holy Spirit our Comforter. In the same verse, Jesus described him as one who would "abide with us forever." Here are some more traits of the Holy Spirit from John 14, 15, and 16. These are all Jesus's own words with which He used to describe him:

Scripture	Traits of the Holy Spirit
John 14:17	The world can't receive him because they can't see him. He dwells with us and shall be in us.
John 14:26	The Father sends him in Jesus's name. He will teach us everything and will remind us of Jesus's words.
John 15:26	Jesus calls him the spirit of truth.
John 16:7	Jesus says it is expedient (advantageous) for us for him to go away because if he doesn't go away, the Comforter will not come.
John 16:8	He reproves the world of sin, of righteousness, and of judgment. He also expounds on this in verses 9–12.
John 16:13	He will guide us into all truth. He doesn't speak on his own but only speaks of what he hears. He will show us things to come.
John 16:14	He will glorify Jesus. He receives from Jesus and then makes it known to us.

There are many, many more scriptures referring to the Holy Spirit, but one of the main ones that stood out to me is in Luke 24:49 where He tells the disciples that He will send the promise of the Father **upon** them, and He says for them to wait in the city of Jerusalem until they become **endued with power from on high**. As we continue on in Acts 1:4–5, we see that, again, Jesus says to "wait for the promise of the Father, which you have heard from me," and in verse 5, "For John truly baptized with water; but you shall be baptized with the Holy Ghost not many days from now." This continues on, and in verse 8 Jesus tells them, "You shall receive power after the Holy Ghost is come upon you: and you shall be witnesses unto me both in Jerusalem, and in all Judea, and in Samaria, and unto the uttermost part of the earth."

In Acts 2, a major experience with the Holy Ghost does happen to the disciples. They hear a sound that sounds like mighty wind, and it fills the house where they are sitting. Then different languages (tongues) were distributed to each of them "like as of fire," and they rested upon them. Acts 2:4 says, "And they were all filled with the Holy Ghost, and began to speak with other tongues, as the Spirit gave them utterance." Many things began to happen through the disciples after this experience including massive conversions, miracles, etc. They had definitely received an additional power from God that they did not have previously. If you look up the word *power* in these and other scriptures in regards to the Holy Spirit, it is the word **dunamis** in Greek, and it means "to be able or possible, force, miraculous power, ability, abundance, meaning, might, power, strength, violence, mighty (wonderful) work."

Umm. Okay, I thought. Well, as far as I was concerned (whatever this was), I NEEDED IT. I mean, honestly. If it was available and God wanted me to have it, then I wanted it because I knew that I desired more of God. Tongues, fire, or whatever—it really didn't matter to me. I mean if He wanted to have me run around or turn flips or turn purple, I didn't really care. I just wanted more of God, and I knew that I needed more of Him.

So I began to pray about it. Daily. I asked the Lord to give me this experience. I told Him that I wanted it, and I told Him that I wanted Him to make me ready for it. More of Him. More of His spirit. That is what I prayed for. I also knew, because I had spoken with my mom about it and had observed that this may include a prayer language (tongues). My mom wasn't very boisterous about this. She was a prayer warrior, and many times when she prayed, she would pray sort of under her breath in this language that I didn't recognize, but she explained it as a deeper way of praying. She described it as her prayer language and that she felt that the Holy Spirit was praying through her and praying in the way that He wanted to pray. Sometimes after praying this way, she would experience more insight from God or more details about how to pray and about the situation. It was quite real, and I observed many answers to prayer. I saw physical and emotional healings take place after she prayed on many occasions.

Well, after about three months, I finally had my own experience. Before telling you about this, I want to say that I am glad that the Lord waited before answering my prayer. I think I appreciated it so much more than if He had answered quickly and right when I wanted it. Also, it taught me that God has a perfect timing for things. This lesson also taught me that He does listen when we pray, and even though the answer doesn't come immediately, that doesn't mean that He isn't listening because He most assuredly is.

I was at a Christian community gathering in my city. It was mostly just a specialized time of praise and prayer for some needs in our community. During the praise portion of the service, everyone was singing to the Lord, and I do not remember the song that we were singing. I was worshipping Him and pouring my heart out to Him in song, and I felt this strong sensation of what felt like liquid love. It went from the top of my head down my body inside and outside. I couldn't tell anyone because everyone was singing, and most of us had our eyes closed. When I opened my mouth immediately after this experience, I started singing in another language. It was wonderful! All I can say is that there was no warning beforehand. The Holy Spirit just came, and it felt like I was being dunked in a pool-full of His love. It was a very strong and unique experience from anything I have ever had. From that time until this present day, I have experienced a much stronger walk with the Lord. I developed a new closeness with Him, and to this day, I use my prayer language quite often, although I have a tendency to pray silently or under my breath and not aloud with it, especially in public gatherings. I do know that when I haven't known how to pray, I have asked the Holy Spirit to pray through me in this way, and He does (see Romans 8:26).

This experience happened to me over thirty years ago. Since then, I have spoken to numerous other Christians about this and compared notes as to what others have experienced in this regard. Some have never had this experience but want it, some don't want it at all, and some don't believe it exists. Of the many that have had this kind of experience, I have noticed that in every single case, each person's experience is unique and different from mine. In other words, no two have been exactly the same. Some have received a prayer language, some have not. Some have had people lay hands on them and pray for this and have immediately received it, some have not. Some have felt a definite "feeling" come over them or within them, some have not. Yet they know that they have been touched by the Holy Spirit in a separate way unlike anything they have experienced before.

I never meant to go on and on about this in this book. In fact, when I felt that the Lord was asking me to include my experiences, I REALLY struggled with it. What are people going to think about this? I am supposed to be sharing about dreams. Why am I talking about the Holy Spirit? Are people going to be even more confused and lay this book down when they read this part?

But you know there truly is MORE of God for ALL of us to have. WE are the ones that limit Him. WE are the ones that become critical and analytical. We are the ones that think we know so much (when actually we need Him more than anything to be OUR TEACHER and teach us!). So I had to lay down my reasonings and arguments with the Lord about why I shouldn't include this part in this book and surrender.

God still speaks. Bottom line. And He can speak in a multitude of many different ways. By His spirit, through the Bible, through a family member, through a dream, through our circumstances, He can speak in whatever way He wants to. So let's not limit Him and let's be reminded as in 1 Thessalonians 5:19 that we are **not to quench the Spirit** (the Greek word for quench in this scripture is *sbennumi*, which means "to extinguish"). After all, GOD is Spirit. (See John 4:24 and 2 Corinthians 3:17.) Lastly, we see that He makes Himself known in this way from the beginning in Genesis and throughout the Bible all the way to the end in Revelation. Genesis 1:2 says, "And the spirit of God moved upon the face of the waters." In Revelation, John, the writer, explains his location in the isle Patmos, and he says in 1:10 that he was "in the Spirit," as he is writing. The fact of the matter is that <u>without</u> the Holy Spirit, we are *powerless.*

So let's begin to <u>recognize</u> Him, inviting Him to speak to us and give us understanding. (The) Holy Spirit is our Friend, our Guide, our Comforter, and our Teacher. And more than anything else, He WANTS us to know Him and to have a deeper relationship with Him. Jesus died for this. In John 17:3, Jesus is praying, and He lifts His eyes to heaven and says, "And this is life eternal, that they [WE] might KNOW YOU the only true God, and Jesus Christ, whom You have sent." Therefore, let us take advantage of the glorious gift of the Holy Spirit that He has given us. A gift that helps us to know Him and experience Jesus to the fullest. What a wonderful treasure and not to be ashamed of! Jesus prayed to the Father in John 14:16, and in His prayer, He says that the Father has given us "<u>another</u> Comforter" that abides with us forever. We so desperately need you, spirit of God!

To summarize: Dream interpretation can be tricky. Ask the Lord to confirm the meaning of your dream to you. Ask Him to confirm the dream with scripture. This will become easier for you as you develop your relationship with Him taking in His Word regularly. Also, specifically, ask Him for a Rhema (now) word. Be open to receive what the Lord gives you. Also, be open to lay the dream interpretation down for a while or even entirely if He does not give you confirmation and peace in regards to the meaning. Ask the Holy Spirit to guide you and speak to you and show you the truth. Be sensitive to His leading and voice. Ask the Lord to help you recognize His spirit within you.

> But when He, the Spirit of truth, is come,
> he will guide you into all truth: for he shall not
> speak of himself; but whatsoever he shall hear,
> that shall he speak: and he will show you things
> to come. (John 16:13)

CHAPTER 7

WHO HAS THE INTERPRETATION?

Shall not God search this out? for He knows the
secrets of the heart.

—Psalm 44:21

WHO KNOWS WHY YOU HAD THIS DREAM AND WHAT, IF ANYTHING, YOU
ARE TO DO WITH IT?

GOD DOES.

Okay. So I know that you are just itching for me to get back
to the interpretation parts of this book. But before we finish with
that, this chapter is devoted to two men from scripture that God
used as dream interpreters: Joseph and Daniel. We can learn much
from their interpretation skills, and I am going to add some insight
to interpreting that I have learned. My hopes are that you will see
with fresh, new eyes and that you will glean a deeper insight into
their interpretation abilities, **thereby enhancing your own**. Let's
start with Joseph.

Joseph

I LOVE the stories in Genesis so I might get a little carried away,
but I also believe that you will carry something away too, so take
this ride with me. Joseph's father was Jacob. Jacob was a dreamer,
and although he was not highlighted in scripture as an interpreter,

the Lord had spoken to Jacob through dreams on several occasions throughout his life. We aren't going into detail about these, but here's a list of three dreams that involved Jacob for you to research:

- Dream #1—Genesis 28:12–17
- Dream #2—Genesis 31:10–13
- Dream #3—Genesis 31:24–29

Please understand that these were major times in Jacob's life where the Lord was guiding and directing him. Bear with me, but I can just imagine that Jacob told his sons and family of these times in his life where the Lord gave him these special dreams. He reminisced and probably loved telling these stories about how God intervened, using dreams to speak to him. But did any of Jacob's children also dream?

Jacob has twelve sons, but the ONLY son of Jacob's who ALSO was a dreamer, that we know of as recorded in scripture, was JOSEPH. Additionally, Joseph was Jacob's favorite son as mentioned in Genesis 37:3. Joseph's brothers knew that he was their father's favorite as evidenced in scripture and by the special colorful coat that Jacob made and gave to Joseph. But Joseph's ability to dream was also a thorn in the side of his brothers as they clearly hated him for this gifting as well. We touched on this a little in an earlier chapter, but let's look further into Joseph's dreams and their results.

Joseph's Dreams

Joseph had a dream, and when he told it to his brothers, they hated him even more. He said to them, "Hear this dream that I have dreamed: Behold, we were binding sheaves in the field, and behold, my sheaf arose and stood upright. And behold, your sheaves gathered around it and bowed down to my sheaf." His brothers said to him, "Are you indeed to reign over us? Or are you indeed to rule over us?" So, they hated him even more for his dreams and for his words. Then he dreamed another dream and told it to his brothers and said, "Behold, I have dreamed another dream. Behold the sun, the moon, and eleven stars were bowing down to me." But when he told it to his father and to his brothers, his father rebuked him and said to him, "What is this dream that you have dreamed? Shall I and your mother and your brothers indeed come to bow ourselves to the ground before you?" And his brothers were jealous of him, but his father kept the saying in mind. (Gen. 37:5–11)

Joseph's Dream Language and Thoughts

Can you see some of Joseph's dream language? Notice that the Lord used everyday things that Joseph came in contact with to speak to Joseph: binding sheaves of grain in a field and also celestial elements. These were daily things that Joseph saw as he worked in the fields with his family. Also, the Lord used numbers in the second dream, and we will see this use of numbers with Joseph again later. In addition, the Lord gave him two dreams—one right behind the other. Both dreams had basically the very same message, except the second dream had a little more specific detail as it included the sun, moon, and eleven stars.

Double dreams and/or reoccurring dreams are important, and we should **always** take notice as we learn in scripture that there is an establishing and a certainty in the repetitiveness. In other words, *pay attention.* Lastly, let's think about the sun (Jacob) and moon (Rachel) and the eleven stars (brothers). Rachel has already died prior to this. What does this tell us? It tells us that we can't extract and nitpick every millisecond out of a dream. Some might even argue that since Rachel had already died, then this dream just can't be "from the Lord." <u>But we know it clearly is</u>. So we have to look at the message as a whole, and the message is that *everyone including Joseph's whole family will be bowing in respect to him as he will be ruling over them.*

IMPORTANT TIP: Do not nitpick every detail (!) but look for <u>the message</u> *as a whole*.

Okay, so how did Joseph **respond** to these dreams? Foolishly, in my opinion. Even before having the dreams, he is already aware that his brothers hate him as they can't even speak in a nice way to him. This doesn't stop him from telling them the first dream, which spurns their hatred on more, and if that's not enough, he tells them the second dream. He was brash and somewhat of a braggart. Hopefully, you and I will take this to heart as we keep in mind that not everyone is going to "share our joy" when we have dreams. It is interesting to see that even Jacob, his own father, rebuked him. The reaction of the brothers to these dreams is to throw Joseph in a pit, almost killing him in the process, and then selling him to unknown Egyptian travelers. I am not sure what kind of reaction Joseph was expecting from them, but I can bet that it was not attempted murder.

Even so, we must be careful to tread lightly in the dream divulging area. Hopefully, we will remember to realize that the reaction that we may get from those around us may not be what we might expect.

Back to the brother's reactions. As if the pit and selling of Joseph were not bad enough, they also concocted a lie about the whole incident by telling Jacob that a vicious animal must have killed Joseph using his bloody, colorful coat (handily dipped in goat's blood) as a reference. So far, Joseph's dreams hadn't gotten him anywhere but in trouble. We do not see Joseph having any other dreams immediately after this point, but we do begin to notice that Joseph is able to interpret dreams for others.

Joseph's Interpretation Ability

Fast-forwarding, Joseph is rescued out of the pit by travelers, but as time goes on, Joseph finds himself in yet another prison (Gen. 39:20–Gen. 40:23). The Lord blesses Joseph, and he is put in charge of the other prisoners. At this time, he is confronted with the king's chief cupbearer and chief baker who have also gotten placed within the prison. On the same night, they each dream their own separate dreams. The next morning, Joseph goes to check on them and finds that they are sad. When asked about their sadness, they respond by saying that they have no interpreter for the dreams that they have had.

Joseph's responds to them in Genesis 40:8 with, "Don't interpretations belong to God? Tell them to me." I LOVE that the Living Bible says, "Interpreting dreams is God's business." So true. Anyway, let's look at the cupbearer's dream and the interpretation:

> So the chief cupbearer told his dream to Joseph and said to him, "In my dream there was a vine before me, and on the vine were three branches. As soon as it budded, its blossoms shot forth, and the clusters ripened into grapes. Pharaoh's cup was in my hand, and I took the grapes and pressed them into Pharaoh's cup and placed the cup in Pharaoh's hand." (Gen. 40:9–11)

Joseph's interpretation:

> Then Joseph said to him, "This is its interpretation: the three branches are three days. In three days, Pharaoh will lift up your head and restore you to your office, and you shall place Pharaoh's cup in his hand as formerly, when you were his cupbearer." (Gen. 40:12–13)

Notes on the interpretation:
Joseph starts by saying that the three branches are three days. So here we see Joseph's ability with numbers (his dream language!) **again**. The cupbearer's dream revolves around the grapes. He interprets the clusters of ripened grapes coming forth and being squeezed in the cup as a positive sign. The cupbearer taking the grapes and pressing them into Pharaoh's cup (as before) is an indication of his

job being restored. The dream was pretty self-explanatory; Joseph just put it all together for him and clarified it with the time element.

Now let's look at the baker's dream and interpretation:

> When the chief baker saw that Joseph had given a favorable interpretation, he said to Joseph, "I too had a dream: On my head were three baskets of bread. In the top basket were all kinds of baked goods for Pharaoh, but the birds were eating them out of the basket on my head." (Gen. 40:16–17)

Joseph's interpretation:

> "This is what it means," Joseph said. "The three baskets are three days. Within three days Pharaoh will lift off your head and impale your body on a pole. And the birds will eat away your flesh." (Gen. 40:18–19)

Notes on the interpretation:

The three baskets were three days as well. Unfortunately, Pharaoh did not receive the baked goods; the birds did. And they ate them out of the baskets upon the baker's head. The baker's dream revolves around <u>his head</u>. The baskets were on his head, the baked goods were in the top basket on his head, and, finally, the birds ate the goods out of the basket upon his head. It was quite simple: again, Joseph just put it altogether for him. I also think it probable that the baker knew his dream was ominous since he waited for the cupbearer to go first and wouldn't share his dream until he saw that the cupbearer's dream was "good."

IMPORTANT TIP: **Joseph was obedient to share a positive/good interpretation, as well as a negative/bad one. He was just plain obedient. This is a real key for us. We HAVE to be willing to hear what the Lord speaks to us, positive or negative, and receive it however hard it may be. Dreams from the Lord are meant to help**

us. But they won't help us if we are not willing to receive <u>the truth</u> of the message that they have for us.

Let's continue on with what happens to Joseph...

Joseph asks the cupbearer to remember him to Pharaoh, but he doesn't; he forgets. A whole two years later, Pharaoh has two dreams. He calls for the magicians and wise men, but no one can interpret them for him. Suddenly the cupbearer remembers Joseph. Joseph is summoned, and he responds as he did when he gave the first interpretations. It is a response that we should be reminded of and take to heart. In Genesis 41:16, Joseph says, "<u>I cannot do it</u>: but <u>God</u> shall give Pharaoh the answer he desires." Let's look at Pharaoh's dreams and their interpretations:

> After two whole years, Pharaoh dreamed that he was standing by the Nile, and behold, there came up out of the Nile seven cows, attractive and plump, and they fed in the reed grass. And behold, seven other cows, ugly and thin, came up out of the Nile after them, and stood by the other cows on the bank of the Nile. And the ugly, thin cows ate up the seven attractive, plump cows. And Pharaoh awoke. And he fell asleep and dreamed a second time. And behold, seven ears of grain, plump and good, were growing on one stalk. And behold, after them sprouted seven ears, thin and blighted by the east wind. And the thin ears swallowed up the seven plump, full ears. And Pharaoh awoke, and behold, it was a dream. (Gen. 41:1–7)

Joseph's interpretations:

> Then Joseph said to Pharaoh, "The dreams of Pharaoh are one; God has revealed to Pharaoh what he is about to do. The seven good cows are seven years, and the seven good ears are seven

years; the dreams are one. The seven lean and ugly cows that came up after them are seven years, and the seven empty ears blighted by the east wind are also seven years of famine. It is as I told Pharaoh; God has shown to Pharaoh what he is about to do. There will come seven years of great plenty throughout all the land of Egypt, but after them there will arise seven years of famine, and all the plenty will be forgotten in the land of Egypt. The famine will consume the land, and the plenty will be unknown in the land by reason of the famine that will follow, for it will be very severe. And the doubling of Pharaoh's dream means that the thing is fixed by God, and God will shortly bring it about. Now therefore let Pharaoh select a discerning and wise man, and set him over the land of Egypt. Let Pharaoh proceed to appoint overseers over the land and take one-fifth of the produce of the land of Egypt during the seven plentiful years. And let them gather all of the food of these good years that are coming and store up grain under the authority of Pharaoh for food in the cities, and let them keep it. That food shall be a reserve for the land against the seven years of famine that are to occur in the land of Egypt, so that the land may not perish through the famine." (Gen. 41:25–36)

Notes on the interpretation:

I notice several things. The cows "come up" out of the river. This signifies the future as Joseph says that God is "about to do this." Of course, we have the number's ability again with Joseph. Also, it is of note that the dreams are both dealing with plumpness/leanness, as well as livestock and grain/corn; famine-affected things. We see the use of both the literal AND the symbolic in this dream. You will find in your own interpretation that there usually is like the pieces of a puzzle in your dream. Processing those "pieces" and bringing them *together* to paint the full picture are helpful as you decipher the message. We see the use of the two-dream situation again. But most importantly, we see that God goes BEYOND the interpretation with Joseph and also gives him foreseeing wisdom to know and advise Pharaoh as to what <u>to do</u> about this approaching problem. We can have this too!

IMPORTANT TIP: Ask the Lord for wisdom about resolving issues in your dreams. He will not only give the interpretation but also instruction as to what to do about a situation and how to move forward!

Let's continue on just a little further for the ultimate finish with Joseph (and this is the best part).

Pharaoh's reaction to Joseph's advice is to choose JOSEPH as the man to be set over the land overseeing this impending project. Think about this. Can you imagine the shock Joseph must have felt after interpreting these dreams, Pharaoh instantly promotes him to be his right-hand man and ruler over the land? BOOM.

Right then Joseph's teenage dreams had to have come rushing back to him. He had TWO/double dreams just like Pharaoh had TWO/double dreams. It had to hit him right then and there. It was a God-defining moment. The fulfilling of Joseph's dreams culminating all that he had been through. And HOW has this happened? All due to the interpreting of *someone else's* **dreams**! Let me say it another way. It was a dream that helped trigger Joseph to get thrown into the first pit, and it was the successful interpretation of another dream that released him out of the prison and into his power and destiny as a ruler! This is so amazing. What an awesome God!

Joseph's success was not from a website or a symbolism book. Joseph did not have a list of what colors or numbers or dates mean in dreams. What Joseph had was greater than all of these things. He had a relationship with God and an understanding that answers come from Him and Him alone.

God had long ago started him on a dream journey and spoken to him about his future leadership destiny through two dreams when he was seventeen. Joseph had many opportunities to become bitter and resentful over the whole idea of God speaking through "dreams" as it took thirteen years for his own dreams to come to pass (Gen. 41:46), and he went through his own literal hell in the process. Yet the Lord built tremendous character in Joseph's life and taught him wisdom and discernment, even enabling him to save many, many lives. He was also reunited with his family in the end. Through all of this, Joseph faithfully served God and allowed the Lord to bring about His plans in His timing and in His way.

One last important note in regards to Joseph: time and timing. You will notice that the dreams that Joseph interpreted for others came to pass fairly quickly. However, Joseph's own dreams did not. They took more **time** to come to pass. Hopefully, this will encourage us as we wait on our own (dream and God-given) promises to come to pass. God's timing is indeed perfect. I have foolishly not waited (when I knew that I should) on the Lord to bring about His answer and blessing in some areas, and in other areas, thankfully, I have waited. I am thankful for this because I have seen firsthand the real blessing of truly waiting on God for His perfect timing and will. There is nothing else like it. And I can only say that because of failing to do so multiple times and realizing the difference. May we embrace Joseph's godly character and hearty obedience to the Lord and to his allowing the Lord to have HIS WAY.

Daniel

Now let's look at another wise and gifted dream interpreter: Daniel.

Jerusalem was captured, and the Jews were deported from Jerusalem to Babylon, including Daniel and his companions. This captivity was the fulfillment of many previous warnings from the Lord and His prophets. Israel was idolatrous, ignoring God's law and committing many abominable sins. Daniel was a godly man of great wisdom. He (along with his companions) was chosen to be groomed and taught for three years in order to eventually serve the king in the palace (Dan. 1:3–5).

You can see right off the bat that Daniel was a man of discipline and self-restraint. He was a man that held his relationship with God in high regards. Why do I say this? Because he was placed in a pretty incredible stressful situation being groomed to serve an ungodly king. He was presented with the opportunity to eat to his heart's content with meat and wine sent straight from the king, which leads me to believe that he was going to be eating swell. At least he would have that part covered. But instead, Daniel "purposed in his heart that he would not defile himself" (Dan. 1:8) with this kind of eating, and he asked for *beans* (!). You have to give this to him; credit, I mean. If I were in his shoes and going through all that he was, I would have seriously wanted to eat and drink good, if nothing else, just to pacify myself. But not so with Daniel. Instead, Daniel asked the head servant to allow him and his companions to have a testing time of ten days with nothing but beans and water to prove that they would be healthier than with the wine and meat. The head servant consented to this request, and, sure enough, after ten days "their countenances appeared fairer and fatter in flesh than all the children which did eat the portion of the king's meat" (Dan. 1: 15). Therefore, Daniel (and his buddies) was able to eat in a sanctified manner, and thus we see his outward/inward discipline and his desire to honor God in this way.

Also, we are told of Daniel's character traits. Speaking also of his friends—Shadrach, Meshach, and Abednego—the Bible tells us that all of them were "without blemish, well favored, skillful in all wisdom, cunning in knowledge, and understanding science, able to stand in the king's palace, and teachers of the ways and speech of the Chaldeans." Specifically, in Daniel 1:17, we are told that "Daniel had understanding in all visions and dreams."

During this grooming period (see Daniel 2:16), he is presented with a unique challenge. King Nebuchadnezzar wants someone to not only give him the interpretation of a dream that he has had, but he also wants them to tell him what the dream was since he has completely forgotten it! The magicians, astrologers, etc. are called in but cannot accomplish this. The king becomes furious and threatens to kill all of the wise men (including Daniel) and prepares to do so. It is at this time that Daniel becomes aware of the king's threat and request. Daniel goes to the king and asks him for time. Daniel humbly asks for prayer from his peers. Daniel seeks the Lord, and in Daniel 2:19 we find, "Then was the secret revealed unto Daniel in a night vision." Daniel thanks God and, in verse 22, says of the Lord, "He reveals the deep and secret things: he knows what is in the darkness, and the light dwells with him." He credits the Lord with giving him wisdom and might and with making known to him the dream and its interpretation. Some important things to note about Daniel's response:

1. He asked for time, knowing that it takes **time to seek God.** We live in a "now" society, but we need to be willing to seek God and give Him time to answer.
2. He was humble enough to ask others for prayer and for help. He knew he couldn't do this on his own. He wasn't prideful or self-sufficient.
3. Daniel did not take credit. He did not rely on his wisdom (even though he was quite wise). Daniel's response to the Lord was to **thank Him** for the answer. We need to be reminded to thank the Lord for the answer before we get it *and* after we get it.

Some notes on Daniel's interpretation:

The dream and the interpretation are in Daniel 2:31–35 and Daniel 2:36–45, respectively. This is a very interesting dream, so I encourage you to read it, but without going into a lot of detail, I want to touch on just a couple of things:

1. The beast was a central character of the dream, but the important part was not the beast itself but its body parts. Each area of body parts was made of a different metal or substance. *This* is what the focus of the dream is of. Daniel's interpretation was that the parts represented kingdoms, and the metals/substances corresponded to an attribute of the kingdom that it represented. **Tip: I have found in my own**

     dreams that it is important to notice the thing or things that stand out the <u>most</u>—what is most "highlighted" in the dream. *Focus on this.*

2.   Daniel's interpretation was not "spooky spiritual." In other words, he didn't start spiritualizing each body part. He matter-of-factly stated the attribute and its relation to the metal/substance. **Tip: Try not to spiritualize things in the dream. Look out for and listen to the overall message of the dream without assigning a spiritual connotation to everything in the dream.**

3.   Daniel has his own revelation in the midst of his revealing the interpretation. In Daniel 2:21, just after receiving the answer from the Lord, Daniel says, "And he changes the times and the seasons; he removes kings, and sets up kings." This was a concept that caused Daniel to give praise to God. It was like he had a revelation of God in a new way. **Tip: When you get the answer/interpretation of a dream, it will feel like a revelation. It will feel like a light has come on and you will have a greater understanding.**

I also want to point out something that few people talk about, but it is important to notice the reaction of the king to Daniel's interpretation. In Daniel 2:46, the king actually falls upon his face and worships Daniel and commands to have incense offered to him. I am desperately sure that Daniel was uncomfortable with this, but the really good part is that the king had his own revelation. He had a revelation of who God is. In verse 47, he says that, "Truthfully, your God is a God of gods, and a Lord of kings, and a revealer of secrets since He revealed the dream." To me, this is more important even than the dream; the fact that the king had an experience with recognizing God in a deeper way.

Let's go on a little further with Daniel and we will see that in Daniel 4, again King Nebuchadnezzar has yet another dream. This time he remembers the dream but needs to know its meaning. (I am not going to list the dream here but read it. It is important to note that it was a symbolic dream and that the dream was about a tree, which represented the king.) The king goes to the magicians and astrologers again. They cannot help him. He inquires of Daniel. The interpretation is found in Daniel 4:19–27. Before Daniel gave the interpretation, we are told that Daniel was really bothered by it, and scripture says that he was perplexed and troubled for an hour. This is praiseworthy to note because it shows us that Daniel wasn't quick to give bad news. He carefully chose his words and even said to the king that he would rather the interpretation be for his enemies than for the king. Yet he obediently gave the interpretation. It is also important to see that at the end of the interpretation in verse 27, Daniel encourages the king to listen and accept his counsel in the hopes that he will find mercy. The king stubbornly does not listen. We can see again that God went above and beyond the dream interpretation and gave Daniel godly counsel to give to the king in regards to the outcome of the dream. **Tip: We have to be careful to listen to the counsel that the Lord will give us by His spirit in regards to our dreams. He wants us to ALSO seek Him for guidance as to what to do in regards to our own dream** *responses.*

And finally, let's look at one other king during Daniel's day, King Nebuchadnezzar's grandson, Belshazzar. Belshazzar is having a party and drinking wine from golden vessels taken from the temple of the house of the Lord and giving praise to "the gods of silver, gold, brass, iron, wood and stone." All of a sudden a man's hand appears and begins to write unknown words on a wall in the palace. The king is greatly upset, and his countenance is changed. He sends for the astrologers, the Chaldeans, the soothsayers, and all of the wise men, but they cannot help. His wife, the queen, hears about all of this and begins to tell him about a man in his kingdom who has wisdom like the wisdom of the gods. In Daniel 5:12 she says, **"Forasmuch as an excellent spirit, and knowledge, and understanding, interpreting of dreams, and showing of hard sentences, and dissolving of doubts, were found in the same Daniel, whom the king named Belteshazzar: now let Daniel be called, and he will show the interpretation."** (Notice how the king's name and Daniel's name are similar, and the wife makes it a point to emphasize this.) Daniel is summoned, but he refuses the gifts that the king says he will give if Daniel can interpret what the writing on the wall means.

Daniel interprets the words, which in essence say that because of Belshazzar's inability to humble himself before the Lord, God is removing his kingship and giving it to another. That night, Belshazzar is slain, and a new king, Darius, is crowned. This king begins to structure his kingdom with order, and he sets 120 princes over the kingdom, and he also sets three presidents over these princes with Daniel being the head president. Once again, as with Joseph, jealousy rears its very ugly head, and the princes and presidents try to find a way to undermine Daniel. Curiously, they can't find a way but devise a plan to trip him up in regards to his committed worship to God. For thirty days, the recompense for anyone found praying to any god other than the king was to be thrown into a den of lions. Daniel is found praying to God, as the princes and presidents knew he would. The king very reluctantly keeps his word and casts Daniel into the den of lions. But God delivers Daniel by "sending his angel and shutting the lion's mouths," according to Daniel 6:22. Although Daniel was ultimately elevated in power, he also paid a great price for his obedience.

The Lord gave Daniel an extraordinary ability in being able to interpret and minister to the Babylonian kings. There was great pressure and struggle during this time in history as Israel was being held captive in Babylon. Daniel knew where his help and strength came from. Daniel was careful not to take credit and not to take gifts. Daniel was also wise in that he showed compassion when the news was negative but still remained truthful and spoke the word that the Lord gave him. Daniel also remained faithful to the Lord when his faith was stretched and placed in the den of lions when he had absolutely not done anything wrong. In regards to Daniel, you may want to continue reading the entire book of Daniel. You will find that Daniel had many dreams of his own, and, ironically, he didn't always know what his own dreams meant. We just won't always know everything, but the truly marvelous concept is that God knows. And sometimes that's where we have to leave it. In His hands. With Him.

To summarize: Both Joseph and Daniel were godly and wise and were superb dream interpreters. Both of them gave credit to the Lord for their ability. Additionally, both of them experienced great tests of faith in the midst of their obedience to speak the Lord's word and interpretation; both of them were thrown into pits and dens. Both of them had enemies. We can learn so much from the trail that these men have walked. We can and will increase in our own ability to interpret as we follow their lead and seek the Lord for His interpretation.

CHAPTER 8

DO DONKEYS REALLY TALK?

And the Lord opened the donkey's mouth
and it said to Balaam, "What have I done to
you to make you beat me these three times?"
—Numbers 22:28

The answer to the "Do donkey's REALLY talk" question is, yes, they do…at least, when the Lord opens their mouth. (Or, in this case, when they have been beaten three times!)

This applies to our dreams. ANYTHING can happen. When the Lord wants to reveal something to us, He can and will use ANYTHING to get our attention. This chapter is devoted to sensitive and some-times sensational things in dreams and their connotations. Mind you, these ideas did not come from another dream book. These are examples from my own life and/or the lives of those I have minis-tered to or shared with. I am sure that you will find this information interesting, to say the least, but hopefully useful as well.

Bleeding—Of course, bleeding could represent an actual phys-ical problem that you may be having, but many times, it represents internal wounds that need healing. When we have had emotional trauma, our hearts need healing. It is very easy to act like everything is okay, but the reality is that we are not okay, and until we experience internal healing from these scars, we will continue to "bleed." The Lord uses dreams about bleeding to show us that we need to address these hurts, bringing them to Him and sometimes also bringing them to a counselor, pastor, family member, or friend. It is important that we take this kind of dream before the Lord and ask Him specifically for the remedy. He would not give a dream like this if He wasn't ready to do something about it. He gets our attention with these so that **we** will become willing to face the hurts and so that **we** will not try and bury them any longer but bring them to Him.

Shooting a gun or being the one shot at—Once again this could represent an actual attempt of murder, but most times, it represents shooting someone or something down. It could be that your ideas are being shot down or you are shooting someone else's ideas down. Also, it could be a defense mechanism that you are using to defend yourself and shoot someone in self-defense because they have hurt you in some way or vice versa.

One example of this in my life: I dreamed about being outside on a bright and sunny day, and I just started shooting a gun at a man that I had just met (in real life I had just met this man). This man was a different nationality. And the truth of the matter was that I wasn't giving him a chance. I had pre-judged him and felt that because he was different, that I just needed to reject him. The shooting of the gun was God's way of showing me my own heart, and He was showing me that I needed to give him a chance and get to know him before making any judgments about him. Guess what? I did give him a chance, after having this dream, and he is one of the nicest people I know!

A love interest—I am VERY happily married and have no interest in anyone else romantically, but I have had dreams of being "in love" or dating other people, both men and women. This can be quite disturbing, but I was asking the Lord about this, and there was one person in particular (a man) that I had had three successional dreams about along these lines. The Lord said that this person was His love interest and that the Lord was showing me how He felt about him! He said that this person needed closeness and attention (**spiritually**) right now. He wanted me to begin to intercede and pray for him. I do think that sometimes we are to actually pray aloud with the person if and only if the Lord leads us, but most of the time, as in this case, this was a hidden prayer between the Lord and myself for this individual. After praying as the Lord showed me, I did not have any more dreams about him.

Sexual dreams—Many years ago, I had a very intimate sexual dream that involved myself and a male family member. This dream really bothered me. The fact of the matter is that this family member and I had a very strained relationship, and we were not very close. The next day I thought about the dream and wondered about its origin. Why was I having this dream? Was there something wrong with me? I asked the Lord about it, and I was **quite** surprised by His answer. He said that the dream was from Him! He said that He had given me the dream to show me that He is doing a new work in this relationship and that He was removing the barriers and bringing a healing to our relationship and that He would cause us to become very close. NOT SEXUALLY, of course, but intimate in spirit and in our communication and in our ability to relate to one another. I was intrigued by this as I had already seen a small difference recently in the last couple of interactions that I had had with this individual. In time and just as the Lord said, I began to notice that the struggle and the general "hurt" feelings that I had carried around for so long toward this person were fading. Within a year, we were speaking regularly with one another and even enjoying fun family outings, which before we had not done very often. I can honestly say that now, many years later, we have a superb relationship, and we are quite close. It all began right after having that dream. The Lord truly performed an amazing healing and restoration. I am so grateful.

I have another example of a sexual dream to share with you. This one comes from a dream website that I comment on occasionally. I shared this in Chapter 1, but in case you missed it, here it is again: A girl wrote that she had recently had a sexual dream about her boss. She wanted to know if this dream could possibly be from the Lord (she strongly doubted that it was). I wrote to her and told her that it was quite possible and that she should ask the Lord about it. I also shared the above dream and results with her. Finally, I suggested to her that maybe there was something that the Lord wanted to show her in regards to this person and maybe she should keep an open mind. She was still skeptical, but she said that she would pray about it.

A couple of weeks later, she wrote back and excitedly shared that out of the blue, her boss came into her office to just chat (something that he didn't normally do). While they were talking, he began to offer some advice to her in regards to a stressful financial situation that she was having. This advice tremendously helped her, and she immediately was reminded of the dream. She never expected that the Lord would use her boss to help her in this way, but she had been praying for an answer in regards to her financial troubles for a good while, and the Lord used her boss's financial advice to answer her prayers.

I do not for a moment think that EVERY sexual dream is from the Lord or that there is necessarily a "message" in all of these kinds of dreams. My point here is to alert you to recognize that the Lord can use these kinds of dreams (and does) to speak to us.

Babies/Birthing—Dreams about babies are very common. Pregnancy dreams and the birth experience are also quite common. These dreams can be very literal, and many people receive dreams and see their actual future family complete with their names, features, gender, etc. But I would say that symbolic dreams in regards to babies and birthing are really more the norm. Again, it is very important that you ask the Lord about these dreams when you have them. I find that people have a tendency to group ALL baby dreams into one category; example: baby means new life or new ministry. From then on, this dreamer thinks that every time they have a dream about a baby that they are to experience a new ministry or something new, and this is just not the case. I want to expand your ideas about this, so please read over the following list carefully. Here are some things that a baby **could** represent:

1. A beginning; as in the starting stages of something
2. An added responsibility (whether you are ready for it or not)
3. Something or someone that will not grow up or develop
4. Being tender or sensitive with something/someone

5. Going slowly or cautiously as in taking "baby" steps
6. New life in an area or even in a relationship
7. Something that needs to be "babied" with attention
8. A gift or gifting or ministry that is new
9. Something that you need to protect
10. Something that you have nurtured or that is precious to you (your "baby")
11. Something that is coming forth out of you (could be emotional, spiritual, etc.)

Also, be sure and take a look at the nature and characteristics of the baby. Does it cry a lot (or not)? Does it sleep? Is it fully developed? These are just some thoughts and aspects about babies to keep in mind in relation to your dream details.

Pregnancy and delivery can also represent a myriad of things. Here are some representations:

1. A new idea is coming forth.
2. God is forming, changing something.
3. The delivery itself can represent timing, as in taking things slowly/quickly and in God's timing.
4. Premature birth could indicate the need to slow down and allow the Lord to complete something.

Death—Okay, dreams involving death are extremely common dreams. So, of course, you can have literal dreams about death where you are being shown that death is approaching. Again, this is not the norm, but it can and does happen. But realistically, **most** death dreams are symbolic. Let's look at some scenarios in regards to death dreams:

1. Death could mean the end of something. It could represent the end of ANYTHING—a job, a thought process (!), a relationship, a lifestyle, a direction that you have been traveling, a habit, a way of life, or a season. It could represent the end of something that you have struggled with (which

would be a great thing!); so death is not always "bad," but many times the Lord is ending something in order to bring about change or to bring about something new.

2. Death **shouldn't** be happening. Sometimes, the Lord will show us death in a dream but it **isn't** that He wants something to die or end. Just the opposite; He will expose to you the truth about something in your life that is causing death that He wants to rectify or heal.

People that you know that have died—I have had regular dreams about different people that I know who are deceased. Some of these are family members and some are not. I talk with a lot of other dreamers who experience this as well, very commonly. My first reaction is to think about what that person represents to me. Or is there a quality about that person that stands out to me, and if so, is that what the Lord is speaking to me about? Many times, the fact that they have died isn't really relevant; **it is more about what (or who) they were to me when they were living and** *what they represent.*

Three deceased people that I have dreamed about a lot are my grandmother, my grandfather, and my mother, and the Lord uses them to speak to me about characteristics of their life that He is dealing with me about in mine presently or something along those lines. I have found in these kinds of dreams that it is important to notice the *details* in the dream and really pay attention to what is going on in the dream. Usually, there is a clue or trigger that points to what the Lord is focusing on.

Also, I have experienced some dreams where a deceased person that I knew will represent something from the past that I am facing now. For instance, the time period that that person lived in and that I knew them in is the primary thing, and the Lord will remind me of experiences or a specific thing from that period of my life that He is addressing **now**. Personally, I feel that these dreams are important in some way or another, so I always like to "sit up and notice" when I dream about the deceased. It is really amazing that you can SEE this person again after they have left the earth in a dream form. So I feel that when God is showing you this person, there is (most of the time) a reason. I have spoken to many dreamers who have experienced emotional healings from having a dream about a loved one because the Lord has used it to express something profound and needful to the dreamer.

Pets—Symbolically, pets can represent something that we love very much. Once, I dreamed about my pet and also dreamed about a teacher in the same dream. During this time a good friend of mine and I had recently had a very bad argument. This friend was a retired teacher. The Lord spoke to me in this dream about my friend and our failing relationship, but He used my pet to represent my dear friendship with her.

Hair—I have right many dreams about hair. I know it sounds weird. It is part of my dream language, and for me, it usually represents an overall theme or even a confirmation about the message in the dream.

Examples involving hair:

I had two dreams in one night where I was trying to move forward in a certain direction but I couldn't. It was like I needed more direction before I could continue, and I just wasn't getting what I needed. Then I had a third dream, and in the dream my hair was tangled. That was it. The next day when I wrote these dreams out, the tangled hair dream was just a confirmation to me that it was okay that I couldn't move forward right now (in real life) because things are just "tangled," and the tangles are going to have to come out and be straightened out before I am able to continue. This gave me peace that the Lord knew all about what I was going through at the time and that He would work it all out, but for right then, I just needed to be patient.

On another occasion, I dreamed that my husband and I were looking at homes for sale in an area that we were considering moving to at the time. The homes were fancy on the outside but horrible on the inside. It was like the sellers were trying to "dress" them up and make them appear great, but in reality, they weren't. I saw someone's hair with curlers in it. This was a confirmation to me that we needed to wait for something better that wouldn't need so much work or attention or "fixing up."

Finally, I had a dream about a precious Christian lady that I knew. (In reality, this lady is no longer living and is with the Lord.) In the dream, she looked very happy and beautiful. When she was alive, she always wore her hair up and never wore makeup. But in this dream, her hair was long, fluffy, and blond, and she had on makeup. She looked so happy! The rest of the dream involved a church that I used to go to, and it also involved a change of leadership with new ministry opportunities. I felt that the Lord was speaking to me about new ministry avenues that were coming for me personally and that would bring happiness and freedom and new changes in my life both physically and spiritually.

Cut up body parts—I have had several dreams in regards to "cut up" body parts, and I have also assisted others having dreams about bleeding or mutilated body parts, etc. There are many scripture passages that speak of the "body of Christ." Christians make up one "body" but with many "members." Some scriptures that reference this are 1 Corinthians 12:12–27 and Romans 12:4–5. I like how at the end of verse 5 that we are told that we are "members one of another."

In light of these scriptures, cut-up body parts can be symbolic of people that are close to you—many times Christians—that are going through a difficult time. Also, cut-up body parts can sometimes represent a "rift" between yourself and someone else and there has been a cutting off of the flow of the relationship, and it needs mending or addressing in some way. I have also ministered to others who have had dreams about family members (Christian or not), and the "cut up" body part represents divorce, death, or some major difficulty between them and the person. These dreams are usually emotionally painful, and the dreamer experiences sometimes real physical pain even during the dream. I have found these dreams hard to deal with but also extremely helpful when entwined with the Lord's direction, comfort, and wisdom. Take these dreams to the Lord and ask Him for confirmation, relief, and healing as He wants to not only show the <u>need</u> for healing but also provide the *answer*.

Vehicles—First of all, notice the position of where people are within the vehicle. Who is driving? Who is in the passenger seat and/or back seat? Whoever is driving the vehicle many times is **in control** or *is driving* (!) whatever the context is in the dream itself. Conversely, the passenger person may be allowing the driver to control and take them in a direction that they should or shouldn't go. Vehicle dreams usually show a direction (forward, back, etc.) that is being taken. Not always but many times. So take notice of the positioning of people and the direction the vehicle is going in. I have had many, many vehicle dreams, and they are extremely helpful. One example stands out and may be helpful to you: I have had dreams of my ex-husband driving me around in a vehicle. His driving represented *his ability to still influence my life.* The Lord showed me that **I** was allowing what happened in our marriage/divorce to still direct and influence my present decisions. The Lord graciously showed this and helped me to be able to face this with His ability, but I could see a clear picture of what I was allowing to happen through the dream.

Houses and rooms—House dreams can represent the actual house that is in the dream, the family that lives in that house. Many times, you may dream about a previous house that you lived in or even about a future house that you have never seen. But, usually, the Lord is "bringing home to you" something that is in your daily life that He wants to reveal something to you about. The idea of "living with" something even such as a habit or a lifestyle or even something in regards to your routine. The dream could also be a revelation in regards to a member of the household and not necessarily yourself.

In contrast, I have had people share dreams of houses with me, and the house represents a church body. There are many, many scriptures that speak of the "house of God," and they represent the church or a church body or the body of Christ, in general.

Rooms within a house can sometimes clarify more of what the dream pertains to. Think about that particular room and what normally would happen in that room. Is it the bathroom (where cleansing, primping, elimination, etc. takes place)? Is it the kitchen (where preparation, consumption, family gathering, etc. takes place)? Is it the bedroom (a place of intimacy, rest, and privacy)?

I won't go into all of the details, but I had a dream about a person that my husband and I work with, and in this dream, this person was in the basement of a past house that I used to live in. (We do not have a basement in our present house.) In the dream, I remember thinking that this person didn't really have any business in our basement and he shouldn't be there.

When I woke up the next morning, I was stumped about the dream being in my old house. This house was in another state, and we didn't know this person then nor did I know my husband then. But this is really a clue; the dream was not about the particular house. The dream was really about this person being *in the basement*. The focus of the dream revolved around this basement. In the house that I used to live in, the basement was a focal point of the <u>house</u> because we spent a lot of time there. Over time, we learned that this person was constantly undermining us in regards to work activities. He was doing and saying things that he shouldn't be saying in places where he shouldn't be saying them. He was not "above board" in regards to our business, and he was trying to keep his activities under wrap, but they were eventually exposed.

Buildings—I haven't had too many dreams regarding buildings, but I had one, in particular, where the building that I saw in the dream was very tall and massive. There were evil spirits involved with this building. I asked the Lord about this dream, and He showed me that I was taking some thoughts into my mind that were ungodly thoughts, and I was dwelling on them when I shouldn't be and that these thoughts were becoming bigger and bigger and becoming a part of my thinking. He said that I was "building" them up in my mind and in my soul and that He was not pleased with this and that He wanted me to repent and renew my mind with His word.

Feet/Walking/Taking steps, etc.—Seeing feet in dreams or having dreams where you are walking or taking steps can represent the spiritual concept of "walking through situations" or having to "walk out" something in life. Too often, we want God to deliver us or magically take something away or give us what we feel we need. There are times when the Lord does move in these ways, but many times, He walks with us *through* the situation or circumstance or season of life, and we experience Him deeper and differently than ever before. Psalms 56:13 says, "That I may walk before God in the light of the living," along with Micah 6:8, which says, "To act justly, to love mercy and to walk humbly with your God."

These are some common dream subjects for you to ponder and pray about. I hope that these symbolism tips help expand your own dream interpretations as you keep an open heart and an open mind. The best teacher will always be the Holy Spirit, so ask Him to illuminate the meaning to you. You will be surprised at His practical response. The Lord longs to aid us daily, and He uses dreams as a guidepost.

CHAPTER 9

YOUR TURN TO INTERPRET

And I will give you the treasures hidden in the
darkness and hidden riches of secret places,
that you may know that it is I, the Lord, the
God of Israel Who calls you by your name.

—Isaiah 45:3

I hope that this book has been helpful to you. My prayer is that you will grow in your relationship with the Lord and that you will truly hear His precious Spirit as He speaks into your life, leading and guiding you. The first part of this chapter is devoted to allowing you to try your hand at interpreting. These are four actual dreams from friends, online acquaintances, and one of my own. I have given some space so that after you read the dreams and pray and apply the steps outlined in this book, you can write down your thoughts and what the Lord gives you. Then you can compare this to the actual interpretations and responses. I believe that you will be encouraged and that this will be a helpful tool for you. So give it a try. Don't look at the interpretations first. It is your time to really try and ask the Lord to help you and *listen* for His response.

Dream #1—*"I had this dream after falling asleep after having my devotion with God. My husband and I were carrying down some items, and my kids were sitting on my husband's stack of things going down some stairs. We were in an unfamiliar place, and my toddler fell off and down the stairs, and my husband ran to get him. When he picked him* *up, he was limp, and my husband said he was dead. I was devastated, and I started waking up, but it was like my eyes were being pressed shut, and I saw this burst of yellow light, and I was able to wake up fully. I immediately prayed against what happened in the dream, but it has lingered with me. I am unsure what it may mean. Thanks in advance."*

For the reader: Ask the Holy Spirit for the interpretation. Listen and record what you hear. Do you feel that this is a literal dream or symbolic dream? Is there a message that stands out in this dream? Record any and every thing. Don't be afraid. Do not be concerned about if you are wrong or right. This is a learning exercise. Give it a go.

_____

_____

_____

_____

_____

_____

_____

_____

_____

Dream #1 Interpretation—When I read the part about "your husband carrying some things downstairs in un unfamiliar place" and then the accident, it makes me think of your husband, in particular, with a heavy load or a load of some kind (spiritual burden?) maybe that he feels responsible for, and the Lord wants to ease that load for him. Maybe he feels a lot of pressure, etc., not sure, but I think that the dream with your child dying is just symbolic to emphasize what your husband feels and may be experiencing. These are just thoughts, mind you, but this is what stands out to me as the message in the dream. He may need prayer, encouragement, or something from the Lord right now. I hope this helps you in some very special way and points you in the right direction as you continue to seek the Lord.

Dream #1 Response from dreamer—*"After praying about your response, I went to my husband and asked him if there was anything that was bothering him. At first, he said no, but then he opened up and began* to share some things with me that I had no idea about. Yes, there is something that has been bothering him very much, and he was able to open up about it. This is a life-changing thing for us and may have actually saved our marriage because I am sure that he didn't know how to come to me about this. I am so thankful for your ministry. Thank you so, so much!"

****

Dream #2—*I had a dream I had triplets. I was having a bit of a hard time juggling all three babies. It was two girls and a boy. I was breastfeeding the two girls and was thinking I would have to feed the boy later. I also kept forgetting the baby boy's name. One of the girls was named Mary Beth, after my aunt who passed away last year. The babies were lying in bed with my mom, and she was on the edge of the bed so they wouldn't fall out. Then we were on our way to eat at a restaurant, and there was a wreck on the way, and when I looked out the window, a bear was standing by the road and was the cause of the wreck. When we got to the restaurant, I was having a hard time carrying all three babies and their stuff, so my little girl was helping me. I kept thinking how hard this was going to be when the babies are toddlers and walking around. The baby boy looked exactly like my husband's baby pictures.*

Side note: my mom (in real life) said she had a dream that she and my grandmother were lying in bed, and there was a baby lying between them. Could the dreams be connected?

For the reader: Ask the Holy Spirit for the interpretation. Listen and record what you hear. Even if it is just one word or a phrase. This is not a literal dream. So consider the symbolism aspect. Is there a message that stands out in this dream? Hint: This dream definitely has a message FOR the dreamer. Give it a go.

_____

_____

_____

_____

_____

_____

_____

Dream #2 Interpretation—I want to ask your forgiveness for not responding sooner to your dream. The truth is, I didn't want to respond because I was concerned that what I was going to say back to you wasn't "comfortable," but the Lord has not let me go on this one, so I am asking that you just hear me out as I am trying to be obedient. You are very busy and "juggling" all of your responsibilities—kids, etc.—that is apparent in your dream. The Lord is using the babies in the dreams to show you that HE knows what you are going through and HE knows about the responsibilities you have, and HE IS THERE to help you with them. It may be that prioritizing is really something that He is wanting to help you with and come alongside you in a special way and teach you about. So take those dreams as His showing you and speaking to you about this area as He is desperately trying to help you with this. The part that is "uncomfortable" that I didn't want to say to you is that in this dream, I think the baby boy does represent your husband and his being "fed later" and your forgetting his name. I think that God is going to show you how to work through prioritizing with your husband (first!) and then the kids, and other responsibilities will fall more into place, and YOU will have more peace. I truly hope this helps you and encourages you more than anything. Now maybe the Lord will let ME have peace knowing that I tried to follow through with this. Blessings to you, my dear sister. The Lord will perfect what concerns you (Ps. 138:8), and He is able to make a way when it appears that there is no way!

Dream #2 Response from dreamer—*"Thank you for being obedient. I have to tell you, as I read your comment, I felt the spirit of God so strong on me that I can't explain it. I began to cry as I read your interpretation. Things have really been out of order in our home lately, and I know this is exactly why. Also, a couple nights ago, while I was lying in bed, I prayed to God to "perfect that which concerns me," those exact words! So just the fact that you posted that scripture lets me know God is hearing my prayers. I'm so thankful for his correction in my life! God bless you for your obedience!"*

****

Dream #3—*I dreamed that I was at a Christian function, and I was talking to one of the main speakers and telling her that she was going to be able to have a special time where she could minister to some young people prophetically. I also told her that I felt that God was going to have me minister prophetically also. She laughingly said, "You don't have to tell me that," as if to mean that she would include me in with her time and that I didn't have to ask permission. I saw myself wearing huge white retro earrings and shoes. I was dressed very differently like from the 1960s or 1970s. The earrings had a geometric design to them, and I had on a dress or a skirt, but nobody else had on clothes like these. They were all dressed more casually. I seemed a little concerned about what others had on, but in the dream, I just knew that what I had on was my style.*

For the reader: This dream is definitely about the dreamer. Pay attention to the location of the dream. There is a central theme to this dream. What do you think it means?

_____

_____

_____

_____

_____

_____

_____

_____

_____

Dream #3 Interpretation—This dream revolves around your identity in Christ and your ministry. The Lord is showing you that He wants you to "be you." He has uniquely made you. You do not have to behave or be like anyone else. He wants you to be free to be the woman that He has made you to be. It's okay if you don't act like others do; in fact, it's better that you don't! The ministry that He has called you to is yours, and it also does not have to look a certain way.

Dream #3 Response from dreamer—*"This helps me so much! I have felt so boxed in. I have felt that I have had to be a certain way as* *a Christian. I know that He has given me a prophetical gifting, but it is very different from anything that I have seen. This frees me to move in the way that God is showing me to move spiritually. Thank you!"*

****

Dream #4—*I was in the dream, and I met a girl and a guy who were in a heavy metal band. Her name was Ziggy or something really uncommon, and they both were very popular and famous. The girl was especially sought after. We were all at a hotel vacationing, and she looked normal with very little makeup on, and her hair was blond. She wanted to do some normal things and not be recognized. She wanted to play golf with me, and I said yes. The guy didn't think it was possible for her to get away with not being recognized. The girl just wanted to be normal and not always be famous. I was determined to just treat her like everyone else. No one recognized her. The girl wanted to talk and share her feelings, but she couldn't really do it; it was too hard for her.*

For the reader: I am going to give you a hint. This is a personal dream of mine. Refer back to the beginning of Chapter 5 and dreams about yourself. What do you think is the interpretation of this dream?

_____

_____

_____

_____

_____

_____

_____

_____

_____

_____

_____

Dream #4 Interpretation—I am in the dream with the girl and guy, but I am also the <u>girl</u> in the dream. As in Chapter 5 and dreams about yourself, the Lord is letting me see myself as the spiritual rock star but He is also letting me experience the feelings and compassion that I had for the rock star girl (and that He has for me!). The Lord spoke to me deeply in this dream. He was letting me know that He understands the secret thoughts and feelings that I have been having lately. I and my husband are (spiritual) heavy metal rock stars. We are different, and we are Christians. We have just recently moved to the coast, and as the dream was talking about, sometimes it feels like we are on vacation due to the different lifestyle here.

I have been struggling since we moved with feeling different and not always feeling like I can just be normal and do things, like play golf (which I enjoy) and tennis, etc. Also, I do not wear a lot of makeup, and my hair has turned blond from being in the sun this summer. I have wondered where I fit in here, and I have wondered what my place is, and, spiritually, I know who I am, but I also want to do some normal things here and have fun. This was a beautiful answer to me that God knows. He knows everything about me, and He cares. He is encouraging me that He loves me just as I am. I can have fun, and I can also be His "spiritual" rock star. I am free to be who I am, and He wants me to know that. The dream brought me a lot of joy and peace.

I hope you did well. And even more importantly, I hope that you have some new tools to use that will help you with your dream understanding. I have to finish up this chapter with an unpopular but truthful thought.

There will be times when you just will not understand. Let me say it again. There are going to be dreams that you just Will. Not. Understand. These dreams will discourage you. These dreams will cause you to question everything that you think that you know about dreams. These dreams will make you mad. These dreams will try and make you question God and why in the world He might have you going down this whole dream road in the first place! These dreams will try and defeat you. Be prepared because this will happen, and there is really nothing that you can do about it.

My advice to you is not to give up...totally. You may have to give this kind of dream totally to the Lord and trust Him to take it completely and do whatever He may want to with it. You may have to be willing to just BE, with this kind of unanswered dream...just BE CONTENT to know that it's okay NOT to understand. This may be the only way to get through it.

Some of you may question this line of thinking. But I want to explain that when you have many, many dreams that you can understand and many of them are life-changing and they give direction and a greater clarity to your life and then you have an intriguing dream that you just can't fathom, it is hard to deal with. Why? Because you feel like you are missing something. It is also hard to deal with because you feel like you are falling short and not hearing clearly, and if you could just get that one more piece to the puzzle, it would all make sense.

I have learned deeply from dreams that I haven't understood. I have learned that I can't twist God's arm. I can't make Him do whatever it is that I want. I have to play by His rules, and when His rules don't make sense or don't go according to how I think they should, then I have to surrender.

Furthermore, I have learned that it is more important for me to care what He thinks of me than to care what others think of me. This is a hard, hard lesson and goes to the pit of my being. But the truth is that I am His. And He is really the only One that I have to please. There is freedom in this, but it comes at a high price. The cost being the "giving up" of myself totally to Him and to what He may or may not want to do with me. But in this kind of surrender comes real freedom and real joy.

You are not alone in your questions and in your frustrations when it comes to not fully understanding what your dreams may mean. Whatever trust that you thought you had in your own strength and ability will lessen and rightly so. It is okay. It truly is okay, and just know that the struggle is part of the journey and that, in the end, you will gain a greater trust in Him.

CHAPTER 10

DILIGENT LISTENING

Call unto me, and I will answer thee,
and show thee great and mighty
things, which thou knowest not.
— Jeremiah 33:3 (KJV)

I find it intriguing that in the King James Version of the Bible, the word *listen* is only mentioned once, and it is in Isaiah 49:1. However, the words with *hear* in them—which include hear, heard, hearing, hearer, heareth, hearken, etc.—are mentioned well over one thousand times.

In the Old Testament, the Hebrew word for hear is *shama*. It means to hear intelligently with the implication of attention and obedience. It implies to carefully listen and consider what you are hearing. It includes the word to *discern* in its definition, and it also includes the words *perceive* and *understand*. In addition, the New Testament Greek word for hear is *akouo*, which means to "hear in various senses" and to "come to the ears." It also includes the word *understanding* in its definition. What this tells me is that God wants us to hear Him, but on top of that, He also wants us to understand what He is saying.

The most important thing that I can write about dream interpretation is that in order to develop this gifting, you have to communicate with the Lord. He has all of the answers, and He is the interpreter. Allow the communication to be 80 percent listening to Him and 20 percent talking. Give Him your ears. Give Him your time. Give Him your limited understanding and allow Him to fill you with His fresh insight and wisdom. He will do it.

Too often, I think, we start off in faith and trusting that God is there and that He is going to answer us. And then when we don't get the desired result, we try to fill in the gaps ourselves with our own ways and means instead of allowing Him to answer. This leaves us empty and unfulfilled because, yet again, we are trying to work out dream messages in our own strength.

I spoke recently at a meeting about dream interpretation. After the meeting, the Lord spoke to me in a simple yet revealing way. He said that it is not the dream's meaning that we should be in search of. It is the Giver of the dreams that we should seek. It is in the deepening of our relationship with the Lord that we are able to receive the answers that we need.

I have found that in my own personal walk with God, that He is always encouraging me. I want to encourage you, too. You are on a journey, but you are not alone, and you don't have to do this alone. Jesus is walking with you hand in hand. He will increase your ability to hear and understand. He will answer you when you call upon Him. He will make the crooked places straight.

I want to leave you with these final thoughts: Isaiah 55 in the New King James Version. The entire chapter is so awesome. Please read it. Here are the first three verses (with underlines) that stand out to me:

> Ho! Everyone who thirsts, come to the waters; And you who have no money, Come, buy and eat. Yes, come, buy wine and milk without money and without price. Why do you spend money for what is not bread, and your wages for what does not satisfy? <u>Listen carefully to Me, and eat what is good, and let your soul delight itself in abundance. Incline your ear, and come to Me. Hear, and your soul shall live;</u> And I will make an

everlasting covenant with you—The sure mercies
of David.

These scriptures provide a beautiful guidepost for us because
they basically say that whatever we are working for and toiling for
will not satisfy. God is telling us that our souls will be abundantly
delighted as we **listen** to Him. Unfathomable dreams will get less
frequent as you continue your walk with Jesus and as you develop a
fine-tuned ear. I have great faith in you, and God has much to say
to you! So keep that journal and pen by your bed and get ready. I
will leave you with a beautiful quote from A.B. Simpson, a Canadian
minister from the early 1900s, "God is waiting in the depths of our
being to talk to us if we only get still enough to hear His voice."

ABOUT THE AUTHOR

Deborah Katherine Smith is an anointed prayer warrior and teacher. Her spiritual gifts include word of wisdom and word of knowledge. She regularly advises on dream interpretation. She has ministered with other women for over twenty years and led a large Christian dance ministry in Macon, Georgia. She has a passion to teach the Word and to help people experience the reality of having a daily relationship with Jesus.

An avid businesswoman, she and her husband, Dennis, have owned several businesses. Presently, they reside in coastal Georgia enjoying gardening, tennis, and golf.

You may contact her at www.kingsdaughterministries.org for speaking engagements and ministry purposes.